Deeper
Still

Love's Invitation to a Flourishing Life

JOSIE MUTERSPAW

©2025 by Josie Muterspaw

Published by hope*books
2217 Matthews Township Pkwy
Suite D302
Matthews, NC 28105
www.hopebooks.com

hope*books is a division of hope*media

Printed in the United States of America

First paperback edition.
Paperback ISBN: 979-8-89185-283-9
Hardcover ISBN: 979-8-89185-284-6
Ebook ISBN:979-8-89185-285-3
Library of Congress Number: 2025943232

hope*books

Endorsement

Oh my...whether you're new to life with God or a long-timer, "Deeper Still" is a clarion call to God's clear, compelling, tender, practical invitation(s) to our human heart, so eloquently articulated in the Song of Solomon. Josie sheds new light on this ancient text, with the benefits of neuroscience, scripture exegesis, and spiritual practices, and illuminates the very heart of the matter—what it means to live as our truest selves, entwined with God's own heart.

Kristin Evenson, Spiritual Director & Leadership Coach

Dedication

To all the brave women who have gone before me, fearlessly overcoming obstacles to live their most authentic story, and fully flourish in the light of who they were created to be.

This book is for you.

And to my sweet daughters and all the women who will come behind me, may you rise, may you thrive, and may you embrace every invitation to become all you are meant to be.

You are seen, you are known, and your story is worthy of being lived with courage and grace.

Table of Contents

The Deeper
Still Prayer

Jesus, open the eyes of my heart—**deeper still**—to You: to Your love, Your wonder, Your goodness, and Your healing presence. Speak into my soul words that set me free to become all You see in me. Your heart calls to me and says that I **am lovely**. You delight at the sight of me and embrace every part of me.

Help me let go of what no longer serves me—especially the limiting mindsets that have been weighing me down—so that I can arise higher with You. I lay the false, limiting story of my inadequacy at Your feet, and I pick up the story meant for me: the destiny You designed for my heart to flourish in.

No matter what comes, my trust is in You. You are good, true, and faithful. You fill me with supernatural strength to endure and persevere.

Help me open my heart to others. May we be salt and light for one another—encouraging our lights to expand and shine boldly, far beyond what we've ever dreamt alone.

And above all, forever entwine my heart with Yours. Grab my hand and lead the way. I will dance with You on the mountaintop, never hiding my light again. I know who I am—and she is beautiful. I know who You are in me—an unquenchable fire that can never be extinguished.

You have my heart, Jesus. You have all of me, and I have all of You. You will hold nothing back as You awaken my heart fully to the truest version of me—the me Your breath formed and spoke into being. The me made to flourish in Your presence.

From here on out, it's You and me—hand in hand, heart to heart, forevermore. **Amen**

Introduction

> *"Flourishing is the product of the pursuit and engagement of an authentic life ..."* – Dr. Lynn Soots

As believers, we're constantly in a battle over our true identity. So when you encounter something that empowers you to see yourself in a way you never imagined, it's only natural to want to share it. That's exactly how I felt the first time I read the Song of Songs in The Passion Translation.

I grew up in church. We were the family there on Sunday morning, Sunday evening, Wednesdays, and what sometimes felt like every day in between. Maybe your experience was like mine. I don't remember it being overtly expressed, but somehow, I got the message that the Song of Songs was taboo because of its sensual nature. So, I did what any good little church girl would do: I stayed away. This was until I was exposed to its storyline in an entirely different way in my late thirties. It captured my heart as the most beautiful love story I had ever seen or heard, revealing God's pursuit of His bride—us, His Church—in a way I had never experienced before.

If you think about it, how many sermons do you remember about the Song of Songs growing up? Zero? That sounds about right. I've come to the conclusion that it is one of the most powerful, transformative books in the entire Bible and must be exposed to every woman whose heart longs for more of God and all that He has for her! As a clinical counselor and trauma specialist, I began to make an interesting connection between the journey the bride goes on in the Song of Songs and what neuroscience research has found to be healing for the soul. Lightbulbs were going off all over my brain. I felt as if God was showing me a secret roadmap—a roadmap that merges deep spiritual transformation with what we know to be healing in the mental health field. It formed within me a complete picture of what it means for the human heart to flourish.

But before these lightbulbs began to go off in my mind, something deeper was happening in my heart. As I peered into the story of the bride and witnessed God's unrelenting loving pursuit of her, I saw time after time how He reassured her. I saw His tenderness and kindness and I couldn't help but open my heart to Him in a whole new way. His love began to undo my fears and expose what I was holding within that kept me from receiving all He had for me. God will do this for you as well. He has something for you here—something you may not see coming but cannot stop. His love is the most life-changing force we'll ever experience. Maybe that is why so much opposition came against me reading Song of Songs for so long. You cannot enter its pages without being transformed.

I emphatically express all that I've experienced personally while studying the Song of Songs because there is controversy around its interpretation. Some scholars interpret the Song of Songs as merely a tale of two lovers and human sexuality, while others see it as God's love for Israel. Many of the early church fathers, however, believed the Song of Songs was a representation of Christ and His bride.

In the pages that follow, we will use the lens of The Passion Translation, which views the poetic muse of the Song of Songs as an allegorical interpretation that validates Jesus's love for His bride. This interpretation writes the story of the perfect love of Christ toward us, His beloved, as we are being formed in His image through His relentless, accepting, fiery love for us. Bible teacher and Pastor, Brian Simmons, explains how he interpreted the Song of Songs in the Passion Translation:

> The inspired Song of Songs is a work of art. It is a melody sung from the heart of Jesus Christ for his longing bride. It is full of symbols, subtle art forms, poetry and nuances that the translator must convey in order to bring it forth adequately for the English reader... I believe the Holy Spirit has hidden within the Song of Songs an amazing story—a story of how Jesus makes his bride beautiful and holy by casting out her fear with perfect love. This sent-from-heaven revelation is waiting to be received with all its intensity and power to unlock the deepest places of our hearts.[2]

This song, God's love song sung directly to the heart of every longing believer, changes and transforms our inner being and moves us toward our truest, most confident, and courageous self. The story that follows paints a vivid picture of God's relentless pursuit of us and our souls deep longing for more of Him. It is, without a doubt, the most beautiful dance that graces the mountaintops—the dance of our hearts entwined with His. There is a grace and ease as we learn to let go, moving in harmony with our inmost melody—the truest song ever written for us.

My hope is that every woman who reads this will rediscover her true self through the lens of God's love and embrace the unimaginable beauty that is within her. The journey won't be without its challenges. But the beauty found on the other side will be worth every step. In this book, the path is marked with nine invitations with your name on them. Some you will want to refuse, but you must trust in the Invitation Giver. He knows what He is doing to bring about His best in you. And the most reassuring news of all is He will make the climb with you.

Faith & Mental Health Need a Safe Space to Mingle

Deeper Still was written to seamlessly marry faith and spiritual formation with the best of mental health principles to form a whole and complete picture of what a flourishing life can look like. A whole person approach is required. We are not just spiritual beings; we are relational, physical, mental, and emotional beings as well.

This book is not a "do this and you will be cured" kind of self-help read. It is a journey, process, and lifestyle. There's a cultural misconception that deceives us into thinking that we can find the right technique, spiritual discipline, modality, method, or pill that will free us of all mental anguish. But the truth is, and the Bible is really clear about this: we will experience hardship, trials, and things that break our hearts (John 16:33). This doesn't make us weak or imply that we lack faith. It is part of the normal human experience and the sooner we admit it to ourselves, the sooner we can learn how to become more resilient in the ups and downs and deeply wounding experiences we *all* will encounter in day-to-day life.

My goal is to help you navigate this crazy life without taking on additional baggage or unnecessary burdens that make being human even harder. By the end of this book, I hope you will understand that, as humans, we all contend with daily stressors, past hurts that erupt into the present, and new pressures and hurts that regularly arise. I want to show you how you can experience emotions without piling on the additional baggage of shame and anxiety. I also want to help you tend to your own heart without feeling guilty and learn how to accept your mistakes without being weighed down by self-criticism. Ultimately, I want to show you how to live with more grace, acceptance, compassion, and curiosity toward your own nervous system, hurts, emotions, and daily pressures—leading to a deep inner resilience.

In the book *Relational Spirituality,* Todd and Elizabeth Hall point to some interesting trends between the two seemingly separate worlds of mental health and faith. They say that "millennials, more so than other generations, desire spiritual growth for the purpose of helping them work through struggles they have experienced. More followers of Christ, it seems, need emotional healing as an integral part of their spiritual growth process." And yet they go on to point out and I would have to agree wholeheartedly that, "the current state of discipleship ... in many churches is an assumption that the appropriation of Biblical knowledge will by itself lead to spiritual maturity."[3]

We are living in a day and age where we are craving more of what God has for us. Yet our minds are filled with distraction, our hearts are growing increasingly disconnected, and our bodies are riddled with dis-ease more than ever before. I will be the first to say that I absolutely love God's Word and believe wholeheartedly in the transformative power it contains. That does not mean, however, that we can forsake our hearts. Afterall, it is God who tells us in the book of wisdom to guard our hearts above all else (Proverbs 4:23).

What we know to be true in the mental health field, and neuroscience can now prove, is that knowledge alone cannot change us. The brain is changed through experience. The journey you are led through here is designed to be an experience with God's heart that transforms yours. I trust that in the end you will have a clearer picture of what it truly means to tend to your inner world and soul. "In biblical terms, the soul (Hebrew: nephesh, Greek: psyche) is often seen as the essence of a person's being, encompassing mind, will, and emotions. The restoration of the soul, therefore, involves a comprehensive transformation that affects every aspect of a person's life. It is not merely a return to a previous state but an elevation to a new level of spiritual vitality and purpose."[4] Therefore, tending to your soul means you tend to all the many facets of your humanity, and not forsake or prioritize one over another.

It has been my experience that we often resist what we need most. So many fears surround the healing journey. So many doubts creep in and keep us from seeing God's hand of love reaching for us, ready to be grabbed at any moment. I trust that once you interlace your fingers with His, you will find the courage to see that it is not only safe for you to be seen and heal, but imperative that you do so.

A Sequence Must be Followed

All journeys follow a pathway. You don't get to point "B" if you haven't traveled to point "A" first. This journey is designed to transform and change your inner being. It involves three separate legs with three invitations to be accepted (checkpoints, if you will) within each section of the journey. Of course, since we are human, we will have moments where we may need to revisit an earlier invitation or reflect on steps we've taken before when new challenges arise. My hope is to encourage you to believe, if God graciously laid out the foundations of this journey in His Word, that He knows what He is doing. He will make sure His hand of grace is guiding you every step of the way.

God's kingdom emphasizes our hearts. It is by receiving God's love that we can undergo a process of transformation—a transformation that allows us to experience first-hand His perfect love undoing all our fears. As our fears are tenderly addressed, we develop the confidence to embrace who God designed us to be all along and live the flourishing life we were created for. May you enter fully into the greatest love story of all—the Song of all Songs—written with your heart in mind.

Love's Invitation

"Draw me into your heart."
- Song of Songs 1:4

I lost her—and it took more years than I'd like to admit to realize it. By "her," I mean my truest, most authentic self. She didn't disappear overnight. She faded slowly, layer by layer, under the weight of expectations, pain, striving, and the unrelenting pace of life. But eventually, I discovered the truth: she never really left. I had simply lost sight of her. This realization surfaced from a quiet, persistent question stirring within me: *Is this all there is?* That question led me into the depths of God's love, and to the discovery that flourishing doesn't come from fixing ourselves, but from letting ourselves be found.

If you've ever felt like somewhere along the way, you lost *you*—the real, vibrant, whole-hearted version of yourself—then this journey is for you. If you've longed for more but doubted you were worthy of it, or silenced parts of yourself just to survive, you're not alone. There comes a moment in every woman's life when the noise around her grows louder than the voice within. I know that ache. I've lived it. But I've also discovered the way back. The truest part of me, the truest part of you, is within us and she is designed to flourish. She is the part of us who holds our fiercest desires and resolves to leap into God's vision of us, no matter how shaky our legs. I discovered that the story of my deepest longings and greatest struggles led me to her—and now, I want to help you make that same journey.

Love's invitation *Deeper Still* is about helping you discover that the woman you have always longed to be already exists within you. It's not a formula or a list of quick fixes. It's a journey—a gentle unfolding of nine invitations from God's heart to yours. The flourishing life begins not with doing more, but with going deeper—with opening your heart to the One who has never stopped pursuing you. He is whispering: "Open your heart, my darling, deeper still to me" (Song of Songs 5:2). Will you say yes?

Our first response is often 'yes, of course I want more' but as we go deeper we discover hurts and beliefs in our hearts that stand in the way. We are all shaped by early experiences that leave behind remnants of "not enough," "too much," "I can't," and "God won't." I didn't want to stay stuck there—and I'm sure you don't either. Along the way, I'll give you glimpses into my story with each invitation that came along. I've traveled a path that God so tenderly led me on, one that has taught me what it truly means to flourish, and I can't wait to be your guide.

To flourish means "to grow or develop in a healthy or vigorous way, especially as a result of a particularly favorable environment."[1] I believe that deep within every heart is a desire to grow, thrive, and live our most authentic story. The challenge, however, lies in not knowing how to cultivate the "favorable environments" our hearts need to truly flourish.

In my experience as a mental health counselor, I've found that there are two essential elements always found in these favorable environments: **safety and invitation**. This is hospitality at its finest—the art of welcoming every part of us. Every heart longs to feel safe and welcomed. This creates the climate in which our hearts are invited to flourish.

One morning, while walking along my country road, I gazed across a field of newly sprouting soybeans. As I thought about the soil that had been tilled and prepared to nurture this growth, I felt God plant a thought in my mind: *"A seed will always become what it was designed to be when given the right conditions."* God never creates an empty seed. He is the Master Designer, purposefully placing everything within a seed needed to grow, thrive, and become what it was meant to be. It's not about a flaw in the seed; it's always been about the type of soil the seed is planted in.

By accepting Love's invitation to go deeper still, the soil of your heart will be cultivated—nourished and made receptive—so you can grow into all God created you to be. Each invitation will guide you in creating the right conditions for your heart to flourish and help you identify what has been standing in your way all along. There is freedom to be found as you enter into the depth of God's love. Here, you will find the "you" that was created to flourish.

To flourish, we must pause. To flourish, we must tend to our hearts. To flourish, we must allow His love to become the very source and rooted place of our life. Ephesians 3:17 points us to this path: "Then, by constantly using your faith, the life of Christ will be released deep inside you, and the resting place of his love will become the very source and root of your life."

She is Within You

What we imagine, we can become. So let your imagination run wild with me for a moment as I lead you in a visualization meant to inspire you to bravely enter the path ahead hand in hand with God.

Picture a woman's silhouette in the distance. She is dancing openly and freely on the peak of the mountain top. So exquisite. Your curiosity overwhelms you as you watch her move to the beat of something familiar, yet foreign. She moves so unrestrained. Nothing seems to limit her. There is a strength in her stature. Confidence oozes from her. A soothing fragrance pouring out from the depths of her soul. Her presence is so palatable, peaceful, calming, and reassuring. There is a fiery desire undenied, an unquenchable love flowing unencumbered. No one who comes close to her can remain unchanged.

But something tells you she hasn't always been this way. You are desperate to understand the secret to her way of life. But a word of warning: when you discover it, you will find yourself saying, "No, it can't be. That is too simple."

A four-letter word holds the key: *Love.*

She allowed herself to be loved.

She too, the one you saw dancing so freely on the mountain top, once resisted. But she found that as she opened herself fully to God's love, something shifted within her. She discovered an open heart was all she needed, and God would do the rest. Oddly, all her fears lost their power as His love led her to a wide-open space of unbound, unshackled, unbridled possibilities.

Where did she begin, you wonder? A voice whispers from within: "The only way you can is by letting God love you, too." There in the distance a path lights up before you and you know you have to go no matter how long or treacherous it may be.

As you draw closer to the path, swaying in the wind on the branch of a tree you see your name inscribed on an envelope. What is this, an invitation? It's the first of many you will receive. Somehow you know it's not just any invitation. No, this invitation is personal. It asks you to embark on a journey to discover the deepest longings in your soul and find your truest self.

Wrapped in a sudden whirlwind of revelation, you realize why the beautiful, free, limitless soul you saw dancing on the mountain top felt so familiar. She is you. This is your moment to boldly step away from the limiting voice of your doubts and fears and enter a life of courageous self-acceptance—a life that moves to the rhythm of His love and wildly flourishes as a result.

Finally leaving the paralyzing grip of your deepest insecurities behind, you will walk into the storyline of a confident, dancing on the mountain top, flourishing bride. Every step of the way, His perfect love will come and find you, showing you how to cultivate the garden He has planted within you. God relentlessly pursues us into our deepest fears, loudest insecurities, and lost places to bring us out into the wide-open expanse of who we are in Him. When His love finds its home deep within us, it is wildly reassuring. No longer doubting how He sees us, a supernatural courage arises within us, and we willingly risk anything to become our true selves!

God is Love, and Love is inviting you deeper still into your heart where the core of who He designed you to be resides (1 John 4:8). Nothing else changes us, transforms the human heart, or sets free the soul to flourish like love.

The Greatest Love Song

Within these pages lies a story that may at first feel like a fairytale—too good to be true, and surely not meant for you. But then, suddenly, you realize: you are the main character. The one who has captured the King's attention, delight, and affection.

The story begins with the simplest of words, "Let him" and then leads us deeper still into our hearts where we discover a fierce fire within that cannot be extinguished. The one who learns how to let Him love her becomes a tower of strength, passion, and contentment that then points others to this life-changing experience with His love. She gives freely what she has received. Just like in Matthew 10:8 when Jesus commissions His disciples to go out into the harvest fields, He says, "Freely you have received the power of the kingdom, so freely release it to others."

What most often holds us back from freely offering what's within us—is ourselves. Doubt creeps in and makes us question whether we'll ever become the woman God designed us to be. But the truth is: the truest, most flourishing version of you already exists within. She's always been there—just waiting for you to see her, believe in her, and release her into the world.

What lies before you is a call to a deep dive into your heart. It won't be easy, but it will be worth it. It will have ups and downs and times you will wonder, "What are you doing God?" There will also be times where you feel the deepest resonance within your soul as if you've truly been seen for the very first time. Being seen, known, and loved for who we are but also fully accepted for where we find ourselves in the present is the deepest healing.

Will you accept Love's invitation?

It's a beautiful call—but it often meets us in a messy reality. The truth is, most of us have wandered from our truest selves in one way or another. Life can leave us dazed, disoriented by unexpected twists and turns, unsure of how we got here—or how to find our way back. But every journey becomes more hopeful when it begins with a promise. This promise is one that cannot be broken, overturned, or taken from you. It will confront every doubt that surfaces within your heart as you take this road back home to your truest self, the place where you can fully flourish. It is God's promise to never stop pursuing you until you are found and fully formed by His love.

Over and over, the Lord has drawn me back to this promise in Ezekiel 34. Tucked in this passage is a gift for the seeking soul, a refreshing river that will seep into your deepest places of longing and fill the holes within where you feel lost, scattered, and alone.

Ezekiel 34 begins with God telling His prophet there is an important matter He must address. God is angry; a righteous anger boiling within Him for His people. The shepherds (kings) of the day weren't doing their job. Actually, they were doing the opposite of their job. Instead of guiding, protecting, and providing for their people, they were using and abusing them for their own benefit. The Lord said:

> What sorrow awaits you shepherds who feed yourself instead of your flocks ... You have not taken care of the weak. You have not tended the sick or bound up the injured. You have not gone looking for those who have wandered away and are lost ... So my sheep have been scattered without a shepherd and they are easy prey for the wild animals. They have wandered through the mountains and all the hills, across the face of earth, yet no one has gone to search for them (Ezekiel 34:2, 4-6, NLT).

That last line causes my heart to sink every time. No one has noticed they are missing or gone in search of them.

Have you, too, wandered or slipped away from your deepest longings and dreams because you were hurt by life and relationships? Have you felt as if you were easy prey to the constricting lies of this world and found yourself feeling lost, without direction and no one seemed to notice?

God's heart breaks for us and how this world has tainted the way we see ourselves. No matter how far you feel you've stumbled from the truest parts of you, His promise is to come to your rescue and remind you of who you are.

Unfortunately, in this world, there is no shortage of pain. Pain seeps doubt into our hearts and doubt confuses our identity. Hurt, rejection, and betrayal make us question who we are. God longs to highlight upon our souls what is truest about us because He knows a doubting heart will always settle for a lesser destination.

There is a battle within between the deepest longings in our souls and the doubts that surface to squelch them. The Holy Spirit has been divinely planted within us to mature us and help us become the gift that we are uniquely designed to be. At the same time, the world is trying to kill, steal, and destroy it. This is a reality that need not scare us, but we must recognize that it exists.

In Ezekiel 34 God provides the sweetest redemption for what we've lost, what has been taken from us, or covered up because of pain. Pause here to soak in every morsel of goodness it contains. The good, true, and only perfect Shepherd steps in and says:

> I *myself* will search and find my sheep. I will be like a shepherd looking for his scattered flock. I will find my sheep and rescue them from all the places where they were scattered on that dark and cloudy day. I will bring them back *home* ... I will feed them on the mountains of Israel and by the rivers ... There they will lie down in pleasant places and feed in the lush pastures of the hills. I *myself* will tend my sheep and give them a place to lie down in peace, says the Sovereign Lord. I will search for my lost ones who strayed away, and I will bring them safely home again. I will bandage the injured and strengthen the weak ... So I will rescue my flock, and they will no longer be abused ... When I have broken their chains of slavery and rescued them from those who enslaved them, then they will know that I am the Lord. They

will no longer be prey for other nations, and wild animals will no longer devour them. They will live in safety, and *no one will frighten them* (Ezekiel 34:11-16, 22, 27-28, NLT, emphasis added).

What was your dark and cloudy day? What moments or events in your life have caused you to question who you are or made you feel like you had to become someone else to be loved and accepted? We all have them. Moments of shame, rejection, and hurt that shape our memories and subsequently, shape how we show up in the world—or if we show up at all.

The redemptive promise is that your Shepherd saw, noticed you were lost, and in your darkest, most rejected places, He came to find you. In the times of perceived setbacks and failures, in your most insecure pools of questioning, He will dive into the depths after you. He will wrap His arms around you and pull you back to the surface. He is not surprised by your doubts. After all, the world has done a very good job of placing them there. He is not disappointed in where you are or angry at your progress. He is just so delighted that you are here and that you are willing to learn how to let Him love you.

You may have opened this book because insecurity, fear, or doubt has consumed too much space in your mind. You are exhausted by the fight knowing there is more in you, yet the discounting and discrediting voice surfaces at every turn. You know—that voice within you that tells you that you can't do this or can't possibly do that. You've heard it so much it feels like the truth, but now, my dear, the ball is in your court. It is the perfect time to open your heart and let God in. Let Him point out beliefs that have been limiting you for way too long and uproot them. This is the only way the deepest truths about who you are can grow and fully flourish.

God promises to put on His gardening gloves and help you rip out the lies that have taken root within you. No matter where, how, or when they were planted. The misperceptions about who we really are often find the soil of our hearts in times when the wait has been long or when those we trusted made us question our worth, identity, or purpose.

God wants to breathe to life what He has planted within you. He wants to take what doubt has discredited and help you see your indisputable worth. Remember, His promise is to never stop pursuing you until you are fully found by His love. His heart is to engage with you so reassuringly that your reason for being becomes undeniably true before your eyes. Then, before you know it, your personal breakthrough will become a path of transformational influence for those you've been called to serve.

So Where Are We Headed?

Every spiritual journey begins with tuning in to recognize and name the deepest longings in our soul. Ephesians 2:10 reminds us that we are His poetry, created with a destiny before we were even born, to join with Him and fulfill our calling on the earth.

Stop for a moment to think about what lights up your soul. What makes you feel alive? What passion pulses through your veins that you cannot deny as much as you try? Who do you think planted it there?

When you allow yourself to go there, to dream and connect with this longing and passion within, what surfaces to shrink you back? Fear, doubt, inadequacy, and insecurity will always come to wrestle with the truest parts of you, making you question who God says you are. My hope for you is that you will fully come to trust that God is good, faithful, and true, and that He has planted something in you that is so valuable you can no longer withhold it from the world.

In the end, the greatest tragedy is not that we find ourselves lost, but that we never let our true selves be found.

Don't we all want a way out of this wrestling match? If so, we must not overlook or minimize the answer. Love, His perfect love, is the way out. Pain, betrayal, shame, rejection, feeling unwanted, unloved, and misunderstood can cause us to sink into doubt and our fears to overwhelm us. But His love floods in to clear out what does not belong and leaves in its wake courage, confidence, and most of all, full acceptance. "There is no room in love for fear. Well-formed love banishes fear. Since fear is crippling, a fearful life—fear of death, fear of judgment—is one not yet fully formed in love. We, though, are going to love—love and be loved" (1 John 4:18-19, MSG).

God's love rescued me from my fears and ways of being that would never have allowed me to become all that He sees in me. His love interrupted the inner dialogue of the doubts that plagued my mind, and He helped me find my way back home to what was truest about me.

Fear will always try to lead you away from what is truest about you, too. It will do its best to convince you that you don't belong on the mountain top. But if you let Him, God will swoop in every time to remind you there has never been a moment when you haven't been a part of His plan. The bride's story, written by the wise words of King Solomon, is a picture of God's ultimate, deepest, and truest message of love, redemption, and transformation. This song of all songs is sung directly to the spaces within you most captivated by insecurity and doubt so that you can be formed by love instead of fear.

While reading this book, you'll be led to the safest place ever known, God's heart, and the result is even more breathtaking. You'll become the love you receive. You will learn to lean into His heartbeat and fall into the rhythm of His pulse. It will bring to life your true self—the self God sees. Fear naturally makes us feel alone, scattered, and lost. His heart is to bring you home, assure you that you are not alone, and equip you to live the life He has called you to. Why? Because He longs for you to be His partner and dance with you in a divine duet on the mountain top. After all, you are a light that was never meant to be hidden, but on full display for all to see. Just read Matthew 5:14 if you need proof.

As you begin, I would like to take a moment to pray a simple prayer over you: Lord, I pray the words of Psalm 25:4-5 over every woman holding this book and embarking on this transformational journey with Your heart. Jesus, direct them and allow them to experience Your plans for their lives. Escort them every step of the way. Take them by the hand and teach them the rhythms of Your heart and how You see them. May they wrap their heart into Yours and know that no matter what lies ahead, they can trust You. Lord, may You guide and guard every heart who bravely enters this journey with You, and may they open their hearts in full surrender to receive everything You have for them. Amen.

Slow down for a moment and reflect on what brought you here to the pages of *Deeper Still*. What is your soul in need of? I encourage you to write a personal promise to yourself as you learn to open your heart to love's invitation. May your words remind you when fears, doubts, and challenges surface of the reason you opened your heart to this experience in the first place and give you the courage to keep going.

Grant yourself permission to go all in and embrace your true self. Accept that the road ahead will at times be messy, have some bumps along the way, and will take longer than expected. But the results of your perseverance will be oh so worth it!

First Leg

Receive His Love: Be Still & Be Loved

To flourish, we must first learn how to receive God's love.
This is the foundation for the journey ahead.

The first leg of the journey is often the hardest—and the most tender. Like the bride, we are invited to learn how to receive God's love, especially in the places where we struggle most to accept His grace.

It's within these first three invitations that we begin to see the bride's heart transform. She learns to be still in His presence and to be loved by His heart—not for what she does, but for who she is. Many of us know about God's love—we've heard the stories, memorized the verses—but we haven't yet let our hearts fully experience it. That gap between knowing and receiving can become a barrier to the kind of intimacy God longs to have with us. God is after our hearts. So we begin here, with the gentle but life-changing work of letting Him love us, especially in the places we find hardest to love ourselves.

The three invitations your heart will be asked to receive on this part of the journey are:

Let Him Love You
Enter His Rest
Reveal Your Heart

CHAPTER

2

Invitation 1 – Let Him Love You

> *"He doesn't shame you into maturity, but loves you into the*
> *fullness of your destiny. He puts a crown upon your head and*
> *watches you grow up to fit it."*
> – Brian Simmons

As a little girl, I loved a great love story. I remember being captivated by the movie "A Walk in the Clouds" where Keanu Reeves serenades the woman he loves outside her window one night. The scene was set in the most dreamy, romantic setting: a winery draped with old school Italian brick and charm. He sang off-key, but it didn't matter.

This imagery cascaded across my young mind, and I was certain this was what true love must be like. She was a simple girl he happened to meet on a bus one day. Then suddenly, all the plans he'd made no longer made sense without her.

The bride described in the Song of Songs, who the Bridegroom serenades, is just a simple girl as well; just your normal, everyday servant girl who has become the spotlight of His song. She's the one He chooses to sacrifice everything for—just for the chance to win her heart.

If you were serenaded by the King of Kings, how would you receive it?

There are some things that soak in for me easier than others— like when my daughters wrap their arms around me and squeeze me tightly. It melts me every time. They are teenagers now, one taller than me, one still trying to be. Their smiles are infectious. Their laughter is the sweetest song to my ears. But it is their hearts that I love the most. I see all the intricate details that make them uniquely crafted, beautiful, and lovely. They have yet to fully grasp that, but in time, I trust they will.

I, too, at times find it difficult to fully grasp God's love for me. When I first started reading the words that describe the bride (every believer), I slid them right back across the table as if I'd picked up a letter not meant for me. My heart resisted. I know myself, and what I know about myself couldn't possibly be put into the category of "lovely."

Nevertheless, I'm learning to receive. I'm learning to see and let go of what no longer serves me. But most important of all, I'm learning to let God love me.

It is simpler than we think. We always believe that it is about doing more. We think that somehow we haven't done enough or been enough, but the answer really lies in stopping long enough to cease our resistance. God will show up and do the rest.

In *Jesus Calling*, author Sarah Young points to the simplicity of ceasing. In the voice of Jesus, she writes, "When your heart and mind are quiet, you can hear me inviting you to draw near. Coming close requires no great effort on your part; it's more like a ceasing to resist the magnetic pull of my love."[2]

I've found myself drawn into this magnetic pull. There is an ease to it as I've learned to surrender to the moment. It is like when you first learn to float. You're not certain that the water will hold you. You fear sinking. Then suddenly, oddly, you remain on top of the surface as the water hugs your face and you let go. You are suspended by what you can't see, yet can't deny. Jesus is asking you to let Him be the water that surrounds you, holds you, and allows you to let go.

The band, Jesus Culture, wrote a lyric I adore: "I will let love find me."[3] Most of the time, we are hiding behind what we fear will disappoint God or make others reject us. All the while, God is saying, "Slow down my love and let me find you. Find you right where you are. No getting all dressed up and fancy—just let me be with you, hold you, and pour into your soul words that will set you free to become what I see in you."

What must we stop resisting in order to receive God's love? There are three areas we will begin to dive deeper into: His love, His words, and His gaze. With purposeful pauses along this journey, we'll discover what blocks our receptivity so that we can rediscover our truest selves. Before we begin the journey, let me explain how to let Him love you.

Open Your Heart to His Love

> "Let him smother me with kisses—his Spirit kiss
> divine." Song of Songs 1:2

Friends, if you get nothing else from this book, please hear this:
we cannot flourish, grow, or become all we are designed to be if we
don't allow our hearts to receive what we need most—to be loved,
seen, and known.

Right from the start of Song of Songs, the bride's journey begins
with two very powerful words: "Let Him." I've been meditating on
these two words for years now, and greater depths of God's heart
are ever opening before me. Song of Songs 1:2 tells us that every
believer who longs to journey deeper into God's heart begins by
letting Him love them. When the bride, known as the Shulamite
at the beginning of the Song of Songs, says "let Him kiss me," she
is not talking about an intimate kiss on the mouth. It is a metaphor
that describes her desire for a closer, more intimate relationship with
Jesus. She is also recognizing the only source from which she will
experience the revelations that will change and transform her. That
source is the healing words that flow from His mouth directly into
her heart. She somehow knows instinctively that if she accepts the
kisses of His Word, something will light up deep inside of her and
she will never be the same.

To let is "to allow or to permit".[4] How often we prevent—even
forbid— the opportunity for God to love us. We feel unworthy and
undeserving. We hold ourselves captive in unforgiveness and allow
our inner critic to always have its say. There are other not-so-obvious
ways we do this too. We block and even prevent God's love and
grace when we busy ourselves, overextend, serve relentlessly without
refilling. We strive harder, allowing the belief we aren't enough or

doing enough to rule our next steps. Somehow, we've let ourselves believe that it is selfish to receive love. It is actually pride that says, "I don't need anything, let me just serve you."

Galatians 5:22 talks about the fruits of the Spirit—the characteristics that all believers have in limitless supply within us through the Holy Spirit. The Passion Translation explains that these fruits are all "varied expressions" of love. Joy, peace, patience, kindness, goodness, faithfulness, gentleness, and self-control are all an expression of the greatest expression of all: love.

I questioned, "What is standing in the way of me being love in all its varied expressions?" Suddenly, I realized the answer. We've all heard that you can't give what you don't receive. The real question is, what is standing in the way of me letting God love me in all its various forms? What keeps me from receiving His joy, peace, patience, goodness, faithfulness, kindness, gentleness, and strength (self-control)? What's in me that won't let these in? What's in you that resists?

This is a question we must resolve before moving on and trying in our own strength to live a life of purpose and meaning. Without first receiving, we will love with selfish motives and be unaware. We will love in order to be accepted and esteemed. We will love in order to get and never be filled.

Open Your Heart to His Words

> "My Dearest one, let me tell you how I see you—
> you are so thrilling to me." (Song of Songs 1:9)

The Shulamite, the bride to be, begins her journey deeper into God's heart like most of us do. She is burdened, worn out, and discouraged. Her inner garden has weeds she has long forgotten and left untended. She is seeking an answer to the question we all ask: who am I and why am I here? But she is not quite ready for the answer, no matter how much she wants to be. She has lived a long time believing something so contrary to what she is about to experience within the chamber of God's heart that at first, she struggles to let it in.

She says, "Draw me into your heart" and suddenly, she is whisked away to His cloud filled chamber (Song of Songs 1:4). Here He begins to tell her what He sees in her, but it is also here where she begins to squirm. Her sense of unworthiness overwhelms her, and she starts resisting. She comes up with excuse after excuse as to why He shouldn't see her the way He does. But the words that flow from His lips next begins the process of undoing her doubting and striving ways.

He simply says, "Yet you are so lovely!" (Song of Songs 1:5). He knows that until she lets His words sink deep into her soul and become the truth that resonates within her, she will never leave the comfort of her self-made box and run away with Him to higher ground. She was made for love—to be seen and known. And He can't wait for her to allow Him to be the One who sees her, knows her, and tells her just how deeply He loves her.

We all reach a point in our journey where we desire more, and all God asks of us is to allow Him to love us and to trust in how He perceives us. However, we often struggle to do this. The "But God" battle begins: "But God, I am not worthy." "But God, I'm not enough." "But God, I am not like her." "But God, I don't have what it takes!" How often I have had this conversation with God over the years and I find He never fails to remind me of my beauty and my worth.

We mustn't let the clanging noise of doubt ringing in our ears stop us from hearing the words that shape our destiny. When you draw closer to God's heart and let Him gaze into yours, what are your "But God" statements that arise in response? Write them down in plain sight. Know your list well so that each time they surface within your heart, you can pick them up, put them in God's hands, and say, "I know this isn't how You see me."

Romans 4 contains a significant message showing that when we take God at His word, regardless of how hopeless, inconceivable, or impossible the situation seems, we become what He sees. In verse 18 Paul says, "Against all odds, when it looked hopeless, Abraham believed the promises and expected God to fulfill it. He took God at His word and as a result he became the father of many nations." Abraham "took God at his word" and as a result, "he became" what God saw in him, even when his circumstances were screaming, "No way!"

If it is so important that we take God at His word, then why does the negative view of ourselves roll so easily off our tongues? The bride gives us a hint. She finds herself in the middle of this divine encounter with God, sitting in His presence, and what happens? Images from her past erupt into view and haunt the moment. Her past convinces her that she doesn't belong. She sends God away believing that she doesn't have what it takes to go up the mountain with Him and become all He says she is. She stays at the bottom, gazing up at what might have been. But thankfully, this isn't where her story ends.

You know that moment in a movie when you're on the edge of your seat, unsure what will happen next—until your friend blurts out the ending? Well, I'm going to be that friend and risk telling you how this story ends.

The bride finds the courage to face her greatest challenges and rise above her deepest insecurities. How? By embracing her God-given identity and clinging to His promises. She discovers that true flourishing begins when she lets His words define her—no longer relying on anyone else to tell her who she is.

What fear or doubt has led you to send God away, sending Him up the mountain alone? It is such a heart-sinking moment, isn't it? We've all been there. I know I have. Too consumed by my voice of doubt, I struggle to let in His truth—too afraid to take the risk. What if I fail? What if I am rejected? What if I'm crazy and God didn't really say those things about me at all?

We all struggle to believe and take the leap, but let me invite you to take the risk and see where it leads. This is the first of many invitations along this steep mountain path. Will you accept His word spoken over you?

Lord, we pray that You take us on a journey into the mysteries of your heart. We thirst and hunger for more of You. Help us to come into agreement with what You say about us along this journey of self-discovery. May we hear the sound of Your heartbeat resounding above all the other voices and allow our hearts to come into rhythm with Yours. Thank You that You never stop telling us who we are in You and opening our hearts to Your healing perspective.

Insert your name below and personalize the words Jesus spoke to His bride to be. This is a moment where you can grow by allowing

God to speak into your heart and lavish you with His love. When you say "But God, I am so unworthy," just as the Shulamite did long ago, hear Him respond:

"Yet, you are so lovely, _____. Listen, my radiant one, my dearest one. Let me tell you how I see you ... Look at you, you are so lovely _____. You are beauty itself to me." Sit, savor, and soak this in. You are beauty itself to the heart of God!

Open Your Heart to His Gaze

> "The Shulamite: I feel as dark and dry as the desert tents of the wandering nomads. The Shepherd-King: Yet you are so lovely——like the fine linen tapestry hanging in the Holy Place."
>
> (Song of Songs 1:5)

This divine exchange between the bride-to-be and the Bridegroom King sets the stage for the entire journey. God's loving intention is to form us into His image—to make us His image-bearers. The reason He took her to His "cloud-filled chamber," the inner sanctuary of His heart, is that the secret place is the only space in which His image can be formed within her. The secret place provides the bride with what every heart craves: love and safety.

I missed the significance of verse 1:5 the first fifty times I read it. The bride's "But God" response essentially means that she feels like a nobody, dark and damaged by life, lacking any real significance. The phrase translates literally to "dark as the tent curtains of Kedar." Kedar is the Hebrew word for "a dark one" or "a dark place" and represents the "old Adam life"—the old self.[5] She is speaking to the Bridegroom from the lens of who she was, not her new identity.

The Bridegroom's response is, "You are...like the fine linen tapestry hanging in the Holy Place" (Song of Songs 1:5). He is gently pointing her to the truth of how He sees her—reassuring her that He looks beyond her failures and into the core of who she is in her innermost being. Romans 5:1 speaks to how this is possible, "Our faith in Jesus transfers God's righteousness to us and he now declares us flawless in his eyes."

The Bridegroom's response to the bride is not simply a polite gesture, like the way we often react awkwardly when someone puts themselves down. In those moments, we may struggle to find the right words, resulting in phrases like, "Oh, don't be silly, you look great," rolling off our tongues. That's not what the Bridegroom King is doing here. When He responds, "you are the fine linen tapestry hanging in the Holy Place," He is proclaiming her truest identity—what He sees in her that she cannot yet see.

If you lived with the truth that you are flawless and righteous in His eyes, how would your life look different? Romans 6:6 says, "Could it be any clearer that our former identity is now forever deprived of its power?" When we accept Christ as our Savior, our old identity is erased and we are made new. Yes, we may still have patterns and habits that need to be transformed, but His cross set us free to become His image to the world.

Therfore, God doesn't see us through a sin-stained lens—as damaged, worn, or beyond use. He sees us through the lens of His Son's sacrifice, which has credited us with righteousness once and for all, for all who believe.

Romans 5:8-9 makes this explicitly clear: "Christ proved God's passionate love for us by dying in our place while we were still lost and ungodly! ... For through the blood of Jesus we have heard the powerful declaration, 'You are now righteous in my sight.'"

It doesn't come naturally to us to receive such love, but with God's gentle acceptance, our hearts can begin to conceive what once seemed impossible. We loosen our grip on the image we are trying to protect. Trembling, we open to the possibility of being fully seen through His eye of love and redemption.

What I have witnessed within the walls of my therapy room is that shame often follows the experience of being seen. We may not recognize it as shame, and many people deny its existence, but a face that looks away conceals a heart filled with shame. Like the Shulamite, we say, "Don't look at me." We all enter His presence carrying scars and wounds we would prefer to hide away.

To flourish, we must face this fear head on and experience what shame has not allowed us to enjoy. *It is only through experience that the heart begins to feel what the mind has not allowed.* Practice is a must if we want to rewire the brain. We need repetition because we have built a highway within our mind to a false image of ourselves that not only no longer serves us, but confines us. And it must be driven out by God's truth.

So why wait? We are going to practice now.

There is a book I love by Anthony De Mello called *Sadhana A Way to God*. It has many rich activities within its pages, but I found myself resisting one. I've learned that resistance has something to teach me and by looking deeper, I can find freedom. It is a simple exercise, but it's not easy. Here it is: *Imagine Jesus standing before you... He is looking at you... notice him looking at you lovingly and humbly.*[6]

What surfaces? Is your shame-voice on high alert? How well do you receive His loving gaze? Or does it not feel loving at all? Do you instead see disappointment in His eyes? If so, look again. God promises to never look at you that way. Maybe, just maybe, the disappointment you feel is from another—a hurtful gaze you experienced when you were younger that you have yet to find freedom from. Pause in this moment to allow His loving, accepting gaze to undo the fears your past experiences have chiseled deep into your soul. Allow Him to sit with you there and paint a new perspective.

We tend to not question the beliefs that were planted in our hearts when we were young. They become a silent, invisible message that forms a false truth in us that we inherently trust. God's gaze allows us to see what we are resisting. He helps us open up to new experiences that our limiting beliefs haven't allowed. The truth is that if we have come to believe we are unloveable, we will see proof of this everywhere we go.

I had a belief that formed very early on in my life: I thought I was the weird one, the black sheep that no one really understood or would accept. I wasn't like everyone else and because of that, I found myself always feeling rejected for being myself. This led to striving to be perfect so that I could prove my worth and avoid ridicule. Decades later, I've watched this insidious belief seep its way into every area of my life, beginning with my family of origin, then leaping into my current family, friendships, jobs, and ministry.

Ironically, my profession as a counselor and trauma specialist naturally puts me in a space where people may reject what I'm trying to help them see. I run a ministry contrary to our culture that encourages rest over productivity. *And* I took a job in an environment that constantly butts heads with my message of mental health and wellness! Even my family doesn't fully get my contemplative lifestyle and my relationship with God. I couldn't help but feel like I was always the odd man out. Whether it is true or not, I felt it everywhere I went.

I didn't realize how deeply this belief had integrated into every aspect of my life until I was sitting across from a very wise spiritual director. I talked about how I felt growing up and the stress my current work environment was having on me and she said, "Stop and listen. Pay attention to all the places where the black sheep has found a way into your life and how it makes you return to your pattern of striving to be perfect." Yuck! I certainly didn't like looking at that. But the truth is that we all have these ingrained messages. Throughout this journey you will have to confront yours as I have had to mine. It is possible—we just have to be willing to experience life through a new lens.

Cultivating a "Let Him" Spirit

One of the first things that resonated deep with my soul as I began studying the Song of Songs was the footnote in 1:2. As I read the words, I became aware of something deeply true, yet difficult: "To enter the doorway of Jesus' heart we must begin by saying, 'Let him'. We only bring him a yielded heart and must 'let him' do the rest... We don't begin by doing but by yielding."[7]

It sounds beautiful in theory, but how do we achieve this? How do we learn to embrace the parts of ourselves we least accept so that we stop rejecting His love, words, and gaze? First, we must discover why we started rejecting ourselves in the first place. What story, beliefs, and hurts do these parts of you hold that won't let His love in? This is the journey we will be going on together, each chapter representing a new invitation—an invitation to a freer you.

One of the greatest obstacles to living a flourishing life is our struggle to love ourselves and extend self-compassion. When we show compassion to others, we acknowledge their suffering and respond with empathy and kindness—not judgment—especially in moments of failure or imperfection. We recognize that these experiences are simply part of being human. Self-compassion invites us to offer that same understanding, gentleness, and grace to ourselves.

How well do you acknowledge your suffering, care for your own heart, and not judge yourself for your feelings? When you are struggling or notice something you dislike about yourself, self-compassion tells you not to ignore it, but instead, tend to it by asking yourself, "How can I comfort and care for myself in a way that will ease my suffering?" We often use shame and criticism to change our behavior, but love will always prove to be a more powerful motivator.

Dr. Kristin Neff, a pioneer in self-compassion research, identified that there are three core elements that make up self-compassion.[8] The first is cultivating self-kindness instead of self-judgement. Being self-compassionate means that we are warm and understanding toward ourselves when we feel we have failed to measure up or hit the mark and we make a choice to not overly criticize or judge ourselves too harshly. Self-compassionate people tend to be more gentle with themselves, realizing that imperfection, failure, and difficulty is inevitable, not preventable.

When we resist the reality that we, life, and others may not always meet our ideals, we cause ourselves unnecessary suffering. Stress, frustration, and self-criticism flood in where grace is the only antidote. As a result, developing self-compassion leads to greater emotional stability. I'd be the first to sign up for a little more emotional stability, wouldn't you?

The second element of self-compassion is recognizing that suffering and mistakes are a part of the shared human experience and not something that only happens to us in isolation. Sometimes, we can feel alone in our suffering as if everyone else is living the good life and we are the only ones experiencing the difficulties that life brings. Self-compassionate people open their gaze to the reality that they are not the only person suffering or making mistakes. To be human means we are vulnerable, imperfect, and prone to mess things up from time to time.

Third, self-compassion invites us to take a mindful approach to our emotional experiences, rather than becoming overly identified with them. Practically, this means we neither exaggerate nor suppress what we feel. Mindfulness fosters non-judgment—it allows us to be present with our emotions without being overwhelmed by them. It's important to recognize that we cannot offer compassion to pain we ignore or refuse to feel. Instead, we can learn to acknowledge our emotions without allowing them to define our identity. It all begins with releasing judgment and choosing to accept and love ourselves through whatever we face.

As I was discussing this topic with my dear friend, Holly, she said something that wraps this whole concept up into a perfectly tied bow. She said, "Self-compassion is like a ticket into God's presence: without it we cannot truly connect with God." All research aside, the greatest gift self-compassion gives us is the ability to be with ourselves in the space where God resides. He is within us, guiding, loving, and accepting us as we are while gently leading us to see ourselves as He does.

Jesuit priest, Anthony De Mello, so clearly pointed out this truth is his words when he said, "The great turning point in your life comes not when you realize that you love God but when you realize and fully accept the fact that God loves you unconditionally."[9] Coming to this realization transformed how I began to see myself and subsequently, what I allow my heart to receive. Learning to let God love, delight in, and embrace me in all my mess, missteps, flops, and failures shifted the story in my heart. I once believed that I had to *do* to be loved; now I know all we need is to *receive* what is already ours.

What is the story you have told yourself about your own lovability? How many "But God" statements arise within your heart at God's every attempt to love you and tell you how He sees you? If you say you don't have any, I encourage you to search a little deeper. If you are human, you've experienced hurt and rejection, and you began to tell yourself that you didn't quite measure up or it wasn't okay to be yourself.

So, I challenge you to pause right here before trying to move on to the next invitation. Reflect on your life experiences that have shaped your story of what love is, isn't, and how much you are worthy of it. When we have had painful experiences of abandonment, rejection, and not being seen or valued by those who were supposed to love us (whether intentional or not), there is a story of unworthiness that gets written upon our hearts. This story raises a stiff hand up against and shoves away the love God is trying to pour into the places within you most longing for His love and acceptance.

Many of my clients have an instinctive resistance that makes self-compassion quite challenging. It is more difficult than one would think to allow in moments of feeling love, joy, or pleasure.

Our hearts skip right by them as if they're a fluke. If you find yourself there too, let's ease into the practice of self compassion through a reflective skill I call "snapshots of grace."

It turns out we all have an album of sorts within our hearts that captures the experiences in life that have touched us, changed us, and moved us deeply. It is also true that as humans we can easily forget them. The beauty of imagination is that we can intentionally bring this album back to life within our mind and relive these memories all over again. The most powerful resetting memories contain moments where we felt surprised by grace, loved, and experienced joy or awe. By practicing recapturing these snapshots of grace, we can actually build our capacity to allow in love and joy in deeper, healing ways. Let's give it a try, shall we?

Find a space where you can sit quietly and begin to open up this album within your heart and mind. Recall times in your life when you felt deeply loved or overflowing joy. Notice the moments when people graced your day with kindness and made you feel accepted or grateful. Then allow yourself to recall times when you felt God's presence, love, or comfort grace your day, life, or situation. See what memories surface and savor the ones that feel most inviting. Peer at these experiences with vivid detail, recalling what you felt, saw, heard, and thought. The more you bring to mind these memories with all of your senses, the more impactful the recalling becomes.

As you are remembering these moments, invite Jesus into the scene. What is He doing to express His love and grace to you? Write or draw out these memories in your journal. In moments when you are hurting, struggling to love yourself, or feeling alone, you can come back here to this page and soak in the healing moments that

God has peppered throughout your life. Regularly returning to this album is one of the best ways to build up psychological well-being and wholeness. This practice also helps you begin to tear down the wall of resistance within you that keeps you from receiving the love and joy you deserve and crave.

Along this journey with God's heart, you may find that you struggle to receive or allow your heart to experience certain invitations more than others. Resistance is normal and often points to a wounded place within us that holds messages of self-rejection or unworthiness. With each invitation you accept, little by little, a new understanding of God's unimaginable love will begin to grow within you and will allow you to experience His antidote to the hurt your heart endured. And the first place you begin is by letting Him love you, for it opens the door to all the other invitations that follow. May your heart begin to overflow with the belief that God loves you, just because He loves you.

Your Invitation to Let Him Love You

You are invited to let God love you by opening your heart to His words and His loving gaze. Let Him love you, all the many pieces of you, even the ones you feel are the most flawed and broken. Let His acceptance flow into the places you reject the most about yourself and open your heart to hear how He sees you. Every time a thought surfaces that fights against the truth of who He says you are, stop in that moment and receive His words spoken directly to those places of self-doubt, insecurity, and fear and hear Him say to you, "Yet_____, (insert your name) you are so lovely to me" (Song of Songs 1:5).

Invitation 2 – Enter His Rest

"Because we do not rest, we lose our way."
– Wayne Muller

ater never fails to provide the stillness my soul seeks. My favorite spot to slip away to is any old dock on a lake in the morning. No one else is up, all is silent, and everything within me can soak in the peacefulness of the moment. I can feel myself taking a deeper breath just thinking about it now. The water is still and crystal clear. Nothing is disturbing the surface as you watch the fog skim across the top of the water. You start to feel a shift within as tension releases from your weary muscles.

Stillness does something to our souls that nothing else can. Stillness with God's heart ushers in peace to our trembling places and clarity to our wandering minds. As my mind begins to clear, I hear things I wouldn't normally pick up on in the rush of my day, like the sound of a bird's wings flapping over me, or the slightest splash from fish swimming around me. I wonder how much we miss in the midst of the distractions and hurry that our lives are consumed by.

One of the last moments I had with my dad was on a dock one morning sitting side by side. Just a month later, he suddenly and unexpectedly passed away. After my father died, stillness was hard to find. Nothing felt sturdy. Nothing felt sure. But what I didn't realize at the time was how the depths of that pain would open a door for God to begin to chisel away at a false story that had been written unknowingly on my heart. I was driven by an unrelenting narrative that kept telling me I had to do more, be better, never mess up, and fix it all in order to be enough. God in His grace gently began to lead me to a new story—a story written by His heart of love for me.

In the days and months after my father's death, I waded through the sea of words he had spilled onto the pages of his journals. As my eyes squinted to read his chicken scratched words, a phrase he penned highlighted something in me I had yet to name. He wrote that he was "soul weary." He was writing his life story, in which he, too, had lost his father early and unexpectedly. He also wrestled with feeling like he wasn't doing enough, questioning if he was missing something. It was at that moment that I realized that the grind of life had reached deep into his very bones and I was experiencing this very same grind.

Months after my father's passing, I found myself knees to chest on the floor, not praying, but weeping. My husband sat at my side and patted my back as if to say, "There, there, it will be okay." But nothing felt okay. I was falling apart. Even before this dark cloud of grief had consumed me, I was ministry weary. My soul was tired of the constant struggle and striving. I was professionally and personally exhausted with a mind full of questions but no answers. "Can I go on? Can I keep doing this? If so, how?" With much of what I thought defined my identity now gone, how was I suddenly supposed to move on? To be honest, there wasn't much movement at first. I felt lost. I remember saying, "I don't have what it takes! I mess everything up!" My heart was heavy with the lie that I had let my dad and his legacy down. In reality, God would show me that a shift was ahead of me.

My husband held me in his comforting arms as I wept. I don't think he knew what to do with the level of emotion that was pouring out of me. But somehow, he managed to utter the words I needed to hear. For my entire life, I'd been punished by the pain of perfectionism, never quite hitting the mark of all my lofty expectations. I felt like I had failed beyond repair. I had disappointed everyone, including myself. But thank God for my husband, who swooped in to rescue me. He said to me, "Josie, you've got this. This is who you are!" I'll never forget that moment. It is branded in the synapses of my brain and has become an anchor for my soul. He spoke truth into me, my true-identity, and it woke up the ounce of hope I still had left within me.

This is a picture of God's pursuit of us. He comes to our rescue when we feel at our worst. When we feel we've flubbed it all up and we are beyond repair, lifting our heads, He says, "No, you've got this, you were made for this. This is who you are to me!" And just like that, we find the courage to begin again, to believe in who He says we are, and to go higher up the mountain with Him by our side. Always by our side.

You Want Me to Rest Lord?

One of the first places God led me to when I felt worn thin and soul weary was Psalm 23. In the most exhausted, hurting, and overwhelmed state of my life, I cried out to God, longing to understand how He heals and restores our souls, and He showed me His way. He revealed the pattern, a sequence, in Psalm 23. It is crucial to highlight the importance of sequence in this context. Specifically, B and C cannot occur until we allow A to happen. So, what is the pattern? It begins in verse two: "He offers a resting place for me in his luxurious love. His tracks take me to an oasis of peace, the quiet brook of bliss. That's where he restores and revives my life. He opens before me pathways to God's pleasure and leads me along in his footsteps of righteousness so that I can bring honor to his name" (Psalm 23:2-3). Did you see it? First, A: we must enter into His rest by allowing Him to lead us away from all the day's distractions and fears into the stillness of His peaceful waters. Then B: healing takes place. It is at rest in His presence that He restores us. And then suddenly C appears: the path God has for us. After He restores, "he opens... paths."

In my experience walking alongside women as a counselor for nearly two decades now, it is more common to see women who are trying to do C and skip over A and B all together. We all long to know and live out the path God has for our lives. We want to see clearly how we are being called to bring honor to His name, but if we skip over His rest and restoration, the path will not be sustainable.

I remember the moment I finally got it—the moment this revelation lit up my soul and I began to understand—that all restoration comes through His rest, and that the birthplace of our true purpose will always and only be revealed in the stillness of His presence. One of the greatest gifts God gave me in Psalm 23 was helping me release the deep-seated performance mindset that had taken root in me—the one that lied to me and said, "If I'm not doing, I'm nothing." As I fed on Psalm 23 for months, God began to write a new story within me. One that said, "Josie, you don't have to perform to be loved. You just have to learn to rest in me."

Psalm 23 never gets old to me. It is the nourishment and reminder my soul so often needs. I wrote what it has come to mean to me personally and I would like to share it with you:

You, Lord, begin all things with relationship. I love that You are my ever-present companion, compass, and the safest place for my heart to rest.

In Your presence is a fullness I can't explain. I'm in awe, Lord, that there is always a place for me in Your luxurious love.

There's never a moment that Your arms aren't open wide ready to embrace all of me.

In your wisdom, You led me first to rest so that I could finally let go of striving for the recognition and significance I believed would make you love me more.

You gently nudge me to the quiet place, to the stillness where I hear Your heartbeat so clearly.

My heart can't help but burst open wide in the presence of such reassuring love.

Your voice drips like honey into my soul as your truth frees me.

It is in this slowed-down space with You, immersed in Your presence that you restore me.

Rested and restored, I am now compelled to love like You!

So now I dare place my trembling feet into Your steady footprint. The path You've laid for me is streaming from the notes of the truest song that has always been within me.

I shall not fear, for You have gone before me. No enemy of Your love can stop me now.

For You empower me and have anointed me to be exactly who You say I am.

Surely Your goodness and mercy follow me, go before me, surround me, and lead me all the days of my life.

Friends, I hope you see it too. There is a path to flourishing, and it begins in the most unlikely place: in God's peaceful, rest filled meadow. Counterintuitive I know, when everything within us says we must perform to receive and be significant. This is the world's message. It has never been God's.

I began to see that rest was where God was leading me to do a new thing in me. Sometimes, there are beliefs and ways we've shown up in the world that need an updated perspective. The false story we accepted long ago in a moment of pain now keeps us far from accepting His loving rest! In His rest, we can learn to trust in the Maker of our path and that He will reveal it when our hearts are restored and ready. I love how patient He is with us—so tender and faithful as He says, "Promise me, brides-to-be, ... that you'll not disturb my love until she is ready to arise" (Song of Songs 2:7).

Letting Go of Performance

The bride in the Song of Songs has worn herself thin as well. She hasn't taken care of her body. She knows it deep down, but still isn't quite ready to admit it. Weary, discouraged, and burdened by the cares of this life, she feels empty and collapses under the weight of it all. She tries hard to pick herself back up and dust herself off. The world tells her she should, but she realizes she just can't carry the weight of it anymore by herself.

She finds the courage within her to say, "No more pushing." Where has it gotten her anyway? All her performing or trying to be perfect has exhausted her. Acting as if she is strong and has it all together hasn't worked so well either. She has been working tirelessly to please everyone, to be the good servant she is expected to be. It just never seems to be enough. She misses the mark so often, most days she just wants to run and hide. The closer she gets to His heart, things begin to surface. Why does she struggle to believe in His love for her? He called her lovely, but her heart could barely take it all in. She wants more but she fears, "Will I ever be enough?"

She questions, "Won't you tell me, lover of my soul, where you feed your flock?" (Song of Songs 1:7). She knows she must learn to rest in Him and prays, "It is you I long for, with no veil between us!" Where do you find such a place? And just like that, He answers, "Listen, my radiant one—if you ever lose sight of me, just follow in the footsteps where I lead my lovers. Come with your burdens and cares" (Song of Songs 1:8).

Rest is His answer. It always has been. It is in rest where we find the nourishment we are longing for. He tells us to bring all our burdens and cares and just come. Don't hide a thing. He knows just what we need.

The bride comes and He meets her in the meadow. He responds in a way she didn't expect. As she hesitantly enters His rest, He lovingly reminds her of her beauty and begins to restore the weary, worn places within her.

It will take the bride many chapters of her life to realize this is all He has ever wanted. All He ever required was that she come to Him fully herself and rest in His love. He promises to take it from there. Resting in His love begins the journey, and it is what sustains our journey as well. He tells her to rest because He knows that in His rest, she will find the healing she needs to fill the shoes of the woman she is becoming. From here, let the undoing begin.

Balancing Our Doing and Our Being

Consider with me for a moment how much your identity is wrapped up in your performance. Who are you when you aren't performing, serving, or helping? When we learn to rest in God's love, He begins to strip away our performance-based identity so He can remind us of our beauty and who we are to Him. The invitation here is to find a balance between rest and arising; between intimacy *with* God and ministry *for* Him. The very thing that can open the door to healing and flourishing is also something we fear doing. I know for me; I feared that if I let go of all my striving, I'd lose my chance at significance.

Balance has always been elusive to me. I find myself drawn to images of perfectly balanced stones all the time, and I wonder, does that truly exist? Can it be found? I am a go-getter, but sometimes that spirit pushes me in all the wrong directions. More often than I can count, I've found myself at the edge of a canyon I wasn't ready to cross. I hadn't given God the time to build the bridge of grace that would allow me to get to the other side safely and I found myself falling and tumbling hard down a steep cliff with no way to stop myself.

All my life, striving had been a thorn in my flesh. I seemed to always be fighting for a sign that I was enough, significant, and that all my efforts proved my worth. It still creeps in when I'm least aware. There has long been an echoing in my soul for more. Since my youth, I've held onto the passage in Ephesians 3:20 where Paul talks about God's power to work in us and through us. There is an unbelievable, beyond-all-imagination dream that is ours for the taking. But just a few short passages before this, Paul is describing what enables all of this to come to pass within us: Love. And actually, more accurately, learning to rest in it.

In verse 17 he says: "The resting place of his love will become the very source and root of your life" (Ephesians 3:17). This is what we haven't done so well. We neglect resting in His love in favor of performance. If we'd admit it, we are way more comfortable being busy like Martha than restful like Mary. Mary knew that sitting at Jesus's feet would feed her soul for the doing to come. Martha mistakenly believed (as many of us do) that performance was the path to being loved, accepted, and worthy. Don't get me wrong, being a servant, running with Him in ministry, is a beautiful thing. However, when we forgo times of solitude and intimacy with God's heart we are teetering on the brink of a fall.

Allowing His love to flow in so that it becomes the very root of everything that flows out is the only way we can truly flourish. The sustainability of our efforts for Him relies on balancing doing and being. Learning how to rest well creates the conditions within us to flourish.

What Gets in the Way of Rest?

Somewhere along the way, the message that busy is better began to weave its way into our hearts. Our hurried culture is constantly fighting against the rhythms that make us well. The world's message has taken hold and it has proven hard to shake free from. The reason why is twofold: one, our culture of independence and performance-based accolades is the driving message of our day. Begin to notice how often the story that you have to do it on your own, strive harder, be better, perform, and produce seeps into the fabric of your day. It has become counter-cultural to rest. And we don't like to be on the outside of anything.

Two, we often stay busy to avoid connecting with ourselves and our inner world, where we encounter things that are difficult to name or face. Within us are things that feel too overwhelming and impossible to manage. Friends, when I said that this is not a journey for the faint of heart, here is one reason why: there is no way to flourish if through our busyness we remain disconnected from the core of who we are and the stories that make up our lives.

The story of needing to strive harder is one I know well. For as long as I can remember, I've been fighting to prove my own significance. I was told a story from a young age that God spoke to my mother while I was still in the womb saying, "I was going to serve him." Instead of it being an inspiring thing, I ended up spending decades of my life trying to live up to this word spoken over me. It still creeps in and haunts me at times, making me fear that I'll never measure up. From the moment I heard the story, it got twisted in my mind. It became a prison sentence—something I had to do, that I had to accomplish. It branded me with fear and burned through my soul. What if I fail to become her? What if I never serve God in the way He said I would? This and many other experiences along my young developing journey set me on a long, painful path of perfectionism and created a deeply entrenched fear of inadequacy.

My soul desperately needed to learn God's rhythms of rest. I would soon discover that God had a plan to save me from myself—to save me through His rest.

You know those moments when you are reading God's Word and suddenly, you feel so seen, as if ages ago, He knew exactly the moment your eyes would grace a verse that would provide you with the encouragement your heart needed? This happened for me when I read Psalm 51:16-17: "For the source of your pleasure is not in my performance or the sacrifices I might offer to you. The fountain of your pleasure is found in the sacrifice of my shattered heart before you. You will not despise my tenderness as I bow down humbly at your feet."

Tears streaming down my face, I knew at that moment something in me changed. I began to see a truth that would free me. The source of God's delight is not in how well you perform for Him or what you do. His delight overflows when you humbly come before Him and trust Him with the messiness your heart holds. God in His infinite wisdom shows us here that shame changes no one, but love always does.

A Healthy Nervous System Requires Rest

Women are notorious for prioritizing themselves least, last, and less. We are convinced our needs are not as important, that we are indispensable, or worse yet, that it is selfish to take the time to tend to ourselves and meet the needs screaming within us. We think it's what we must do, but it is not without consequence to our bodies. Dr. Gabor Mate paints a grim picture when he states that "women bear 80% of the autoimmune diseases."[2] These are diseases in which the immune system attacks the body—attacks itself.

Why is this so? What are the underlying reasons that women tend to suffer more from chronic disease and even cancers? Our bodies carry the story of neglect. Our culture hasn't helped much. We are conditioned that "good girls" suppress their healthy anger (yes, anger can be healthy) and that there should be no limit to our giving. So, we become compulsively concerned about meeting the needs of others and experience praise when we neglect our own. We take responsibility that isn't ours and God forbid we ever disappoint anyone.

Women are also notorious for disliking their bodies. We are so focused on the perfect body and the perfect appearance that the messages we are sending to the body we reside in, aren't lovely ones. No wonder our bodies are attacking themselves!

I used to go into school systems and help stressed-out, burnt-out teachers build resilience. Education carries one of the highest burnout rates of all occupations. Even with the stats screaming that "something has to give," many of the teachers I spoke with still found it hard to admit their need. Knowing this is a common reaction, where do you think I began? First, with validation. I made it okay to not be okay. Then, and only then, were their ears opened. When we are worried about being judged for not being strong enough or fearing people will think we don't have it all together, we can't be real. But in denial we cannot heal, thrive, or even come remotely near flourishing.

Once I had created an atmosphere of openness and acceptance where we all could see that everyone in the room was in the same boat, true understanding could begin. I taught about how our nervous system operates and what it requires to be well. One of the phrases I loved to say was, "It is an exposure issue, not a character issue." What did I mean?

We are exposed to things our nervous systems struggle to digest on a daily basis. This life is one big distraction constantly pulling at us, pouring fear, stress, and overwhelm into our bodies. And we just keep going unaware. Authors Emily and Amelia Nagoski in the book *Burnout: The Secret to Unlocking the Stress Cycle* discuss the difference between stress and stressors: They highlight an important distinction when they state, "Just because you've dealt with the stressor doesn't mean you've dealt with the stress itself."[3]

Stress is not our biggest problem; it is the way we deal (or don't deal) with it that matters most. Stressors, things that create stress within us, will always be a part of life. When we experience them, there is a corresponding stress response that happens within our bodies. This stress response is a physical one—you can't just talk your way out of stress. Stress was designed to cause action, to flee or fight a threat, and when we shut it down, deny, or ignore it, all we do is trap it in our bodies. The Nagoski sisters point us to a key element of health and well-being that leads to more resilience in our nervous systems: "While you're managing the day's stressors, your body is managing the day's stress, and it is absolutely essential to your well-being–the way sleeping and eating are absolutely essential–that you give your body the resources it needs to complete the stress response cycles that have been activated."[4]

How is this accomplished? Their research points to seven ways we can be intentional about completing the stress response cycle that has been initiated within our bodies and increasing our overall resilience. The first and most efficient way is physical activity or movement. Get your body moving so that the stress chemicals that are released can move through and out of your body. They also found that breathing, connecting socially, laughter, affection, crying, and creative expression all allow your stress response cycle to complete.

When I think about the above ways you can complete your stress response cycle, they all have a common theme and a reason they work. They all create a sense of safety within our nervous system. The stress response initiates because the body has determined we are under some form of threat. Therefore, creating a sense of safety calms this response within us and allows our thinking brain to come back online. It really does come down to this: doing intentional actions that create a sense of safety resets you, not telling yourself to get over it or just calm down. That never works. Your body doesn't use words, it speaks the language of the senses.

Sending cues to your body that you are safe allows your brain to spin a different story.

Of course, when there's an actual tiger nearby, we need our brain to recognize the threat and respond accordingly. But in our modern-day world, that same fight-or-flight response can be triggered by much less—like a negative comment on social media or a mistake at work. Our bodies react as if there's real danger, even though there's no tiger prowling through the office. The difference is, we know to physically respond to a real threat, but we tend to suppress or ignore our physiological reactions when the stressor is psychological or emotional.

What's more, when we're in a stressed state, our brain can misinterpret signals from our environment, our bodies, and our relationships. We're more likely to see threat and danger, even where none exists, because our brain and nervous system are wired for survival. But this survival mode can keep us stuck in reactivity—trapped in the stress response—rather than helping us move through it and return to a place of safety and calm.

Ultimately, our bodies don't have to carry the story of neglect any longer. They can carry the story of resilience. What that requires is giving ourselves permission without guilt to rest and tend to what our bodies need with a sense of tenderness and compassion. Let's be counter-cultural and give ourselves not only what our bodies deserve, but what is absolutely essential for our well-being.

Where to Begin – Creating Margin with the 3 S's of Rest

Our hearts are craving a type of rest the world can never provide. Learning to intentionally carve out space for the disciplines of stillness, silence, and solitude is a challenge for all of us. There are so many forces that come against us entering God's rest, and most notably are the forces within ourselves that resist it.

When I began this journey for myself, I started with small snippets of practice. I learned how to be still, quiet my soul, and pull away from the day's distractions to get alone with God. The voice of my inner critic was relentless at first, shouting, "but you aren't being productive!" Ironically, I found that when I created space for rest, I was actually more productive than if I didn't.

This was a foreign way of being for me. The desire was there, but the "how" was unclear. My thirst to understand how to intentionally live this lifestyle of rest God was calling me to was insatiable. I fell in love with all of Ruth Haley Barton's books on the topic. The one I am most explicitly gleaming from here is her book *Invitation to Solitude and Silence*. She eloquently expands on the lost art of these spiritual disciplines so beautifully. Ruth describes solitude and silence this way:

> The invitation to solitude and silence is just that. It is an invitation to enter more deeply into the intimacy of relationship with the One who waits just outside the noise and busyness of our lives. It is an invitation to communication and communion with the One who is always present even when our awareness has been dulled by distraction. It is an invitation to the adventure of spiritual transformation in the deepest places of our being, an adventure that will result in greater freedom and authenticity and surrender to God than we have yet experienced.[5]

You see the word "invitation" all throughout this small description. You are being invited into the most life-changing experience you can ever have on this earth. In the last two decades as a counselor who specializes in the healing of trauma, there is no method or approach that even comes close. And I am a firm believer in therapy and what it can provide. But I am convinced, all healing is born in rest–in the heart that learns to rest in His love.

It is the starting place for true transformation and change within the human heart and I would say it is the main reason the enemy of our souls has used distraction, busyness, and hurry as one of his main tactics to keep us from it. Sometimes practices can seem so simple that we dismiss them, or maybe, we are afraid to peer inside our hearts and so we avoid them unconsciously. Don't forsake the simplicity yet profoundness of getting still, getting quiet, and getting alone with your heart in God's presence. How often do you let everything go quiet? Silence invites revelation—because it's in the quiet that we can truly hear the heart of God.

Here's a great practice to add to your life that I like to call *resetting silence*: The challenge is to begin or end your day for the next week with five minutes of silence. You can ease into this slowly, by trying a couple minutes at a time, or reading a Scripture first to just sit with. This practice may seem simple, but it is not easy for most people, especially at first.

Begin by setting the stage to avoid distraction by settling into a space that is soothing for you. You may notice it is easier if you close your eyes or gaze softly in the distance. Take a moment to slow-down, breathe deeply, sit comfortably, and begin with this simple prayer: "Lord, create space in my soul for more of You. Let Your voice break through all the noise within me and around me. Help me to be still in the silence of Your presence and listen for Your heart to speak to me. May all that is in me settle into the tenderness of who You want to be for me in this moment."

After five minutes have passed, notice how you experienced the silence and what revelation, if any, may have surfaced. This exercise when practiced regularly will help you become more present in your day and aware of God all around you.

Soul Rest – What Our Hearts Are Craving

True rest, or what I call soul rest, is the place of encounter with God's heart. The unfortunate result of a busy, productivity-driven culture is that these precious moments of encounter are rare. Our souls are weary because we have lost the art of connecting heart to heart with God. Psalm 25:14 tells us, "There's a private place reserved for the lovers of God, where they sit near him and receive the revelation-secrets of his promises." There is a private place reserved for us and yet, in the busyness of our day, we often miss it. We are too distracted, too busy to recognize when He is speaking and trying to connect with our heart.

We are frazzled, overwhelmed, confused, and disheartened because we are undernourished. Our souls are thirsty for more of God, and He is gently asking us to make space in our day to consume what He is trying to give us. Jesus calls to us saying:

> Are you tired? Worn Out? Burned out on religion?
> Come to me. Get away with me and you'll recover
> your life. I'll show you how to take a real rest. Walk
> with me and work with me—watch how I do it.
> Learn the unforced rhythms of grace. I won't lay
> anything heavy or ill-fitting on you. Keep company
> with me and you'll learn to live freely and lightly
> (Matthew 11:28-30, MSG).

I want to learn to live freely and lightly, don't you? May we all make more space in our day to slow down, let go, and just soak in His presence. Why not start right now? Here is your invitation.

Your Invitation to Enter His Rest

You are invited to fully rest in His love for you and be easy for a moment. No more striving, no more fighting for significance. Allow God to silence the voice within you that says your only value is in what you do and in how you perform. Let His presence restore you and reassure you that you are enough as you are. Hear Him say these words to your weary heart: "Listen, my radiant one—If you ever lose sight of me, just follow in my footsteps where I lead my lovers. Come with your burdens and cares" (Song of Songs 1:8)

CHAPTER

4

Invitation 3 –
Reveal Your Heart

*"The willingness to see ourselves as we are and name it in God's
presence is at the very heart of the spiritual journey."*
— Ruth Haley Barton

I had just taken a major leap into the unknown. I left a lucrative salary behind to put my health first and pursue the stirring within my heart. In my head I was saying, "I am so happy, so content. This is the best decision I could've ever made." Yet within me, there was a mismatch occurring between my head and my heart. My body was telling a completely different story, one of tension and unease.

So what did I do? I got still and went within. I pulled out my journal and just let my thoughts flow. No editing, no pretty phrases needed. Just raw honesty. It turns out there were a lot of emotions whirling within that I wasn't allowing myself to see and name. I was blinded by a desire to prove my faith was strong; to whom exactly, I don't know. I wasn't being honest about the turmoil I was experiencing. As I peered within, I realized my heart contained a lot of worry about finances, how this decision would impact my girls, and what we could potentially miss out on. Penned on my journal pages were deep disappointments and thoughts of unfairness that led me to acknowledge how my heart was hurting. A question seemed to surface out of nowhere as I asked, "Lord, why does it seem that those who sacrifice the most for You are also the ones who miss out the most?"

When you pause and truly get honest with your heart, it can be surprising—even unsettling—what you find. In the world of psychology, there's a term for the tendency to gloss over pain: **toxic positivity**.[2] Unfortunately, this mindset often seeps into faith circles, where there's a subtle pressure to "stay grateful" or "focus on the good" at all times. But bypassing our pain doesn't heal it. Our hearts need validation. We need to know it's okay to feel what we feel—to bring those raw emotions into the light of God's presence without shame. The goal isn't to stay stuck in sorrow or anger, but to tend to what's real. When we allow ourselves to fully feel and name how life is impacting us, we begin to understand what our emotions are trying to show us. From there, we can respond with compassion and care, meeting the needs underneath the emotion—just as God so tenderly does with us.

One simple way we can begin to shift away from toxic positivity and move toward a more validating posture—both with ourselves and others—is by changing how we speak. Instead of saying, "It could be worse," try, "Of course you would feel that way." Which one feels more soothing to your soul? Acknowledging our experiences is a sacred gift we offer ourselves and others. After all, God desires an honest heart so He can tend to what's truly there. What we hide cannot be healed.

An Honest Heart Can Flourish

The hallmark of good therapy is helping people get honest about the impact their life experiences have had on them. Not revealing what is in our hearts is one of the main reasons we stay stuck. It makes sense—who says, "Yes, sign me up!" when asked to peer into the painful parts of their story? Especially when the story carries with it a wave of strong emotions. Believe me, as a mental health counselor, I get it. It is one of the hardest things I am up against in walking alongside others.

My job as a counselor is to create a quiet, inviting, and trustworthy space: my client's job is to speak their truth. In the tender moments of letting my own heart be seen, I have found that God is a master at this. He is so inviting and trustworthy with anything I bring to Him. We can trust that there is a truer self waiting to be rescued and that God will go in search for her with us, bringing her to life before our eyes.

So, where to begin? To reveal your heart, you must enter your heart. You can't critique it from the mind and expect it to be honest. It's the honest heart that flourishes.

Why is "fake it till you make it" so enticing then? I would venture to say that somewhere along the way for every striving Christian, we received some version of this message: "If your faith was strong enough, you wouldn't struggle." This causes us to put on a fake mask of happiness. We say, "God won't give me more than I can handle" and act as if nothing phases us. Then our faith becomes a barrier to our authenticity. It is hard to remain authentic when we live in a world that tells us we must be perfect to be pleasing, always have a smile on our face, and that if our faith were strong enough we wouldn't doubt what God was doing.

When we don't feel safe, we will give up our authenticity every time for the sake of belonging. We see this play out in the story of the bride in Song of Songs as well. After entering God's rest, the bride begins to feel this struggle with faith and authenticity within her own soul. In a raw and honest moment, looking over her life, she realizes that somewhere along the way she forgot to take care of herself, and it left her feeling lost, confused, and exhausted. She had been serving selflessly, yet failed to tend to the vineyard within her own soul (Song of Songs 1:6). She is weary, burdened, hurting, but on she goes doing what is expected of her. She longs for something, but struggles to name it because she abandoned her needs long ago. Within her, she senses something is missing that all her striving has failed to fill. There is an emptiness and if she is to accept His invitation to go deeper still into her heart, she can no longer deny that there are things that must be tended to within her—things she must name and turn to with compassion.

It is interesting to me that we so often seek God expecting and hoping that He will immediately open doors and call us into ministry. But one of the sweetest moments along this entire journey with God's heart we see right here. Instead of leading the bride to serve others, God took her deeper into her own heart, into the hidden garden within her soul overgrown with doubt and fear. As she entered, the bride was confronted with all the parts of herself she had neglected—the dreams she had buried and the fears she had allowed to take root.

The bride begins to realize she can't hide and be found at the same time. She can't wear a mask and be fully seen. His rest was so inviting, loving, and accepting. It allowed her to let down her guard. In the stillness of His presence and at rest in His love, her heart feels safe to heal and reveal what is there. She begins to acknowledge things she never has before. Not just the pain and hurts she has experienced, but now something new is coming alive in her. She is beginning to feel a stirring, rhythm, and heartbeat pulsing within her. In the silence, she hears it now: the song of her truest longings and passions and her need for more of Him. She is willing to finally name her needs and desires out loud and look deeper at what she hasn't tended to so that her heart is open to what God wants to cultivate within her.

In a moment of desperation the bride says, "It is you I long for, with no veil between us!" (Song of Songs 1:7). She wants nothing to be in the way of her growing closer to the Bridegroom, but she doesn't know how to allow that to happen. The Bridegroom calls back to her as He continues to tend to this dance between her insecurities and His view of her. He opens His arms, spins her around, and responds, "Listen, my radiant one—if you ever lose sight of me, just follow in my footsteps where I lead my lovers" (Song of Songs 1:8). He calls her to this safe space with Him before she has made any changes. She hasn't fixed her flaws or tidied herself up. She has just decided there is nothing left but to be transparent so that she can be fully seen and fully known.

The bride begins to feel the heavy weight of her inadequacies and wants to shy away, but together they enter her heart and begin to uproot what was never meant to be there. She begins to discover hidden strengths and forgotten dreams as she says, "Now he comes closer, even to the places where I hide. He gazes into my soul, peering through the portal as he blossoms within my heart. The one I love calls to me" (Song of Songs 2:9-10).

In the bride's story and ours as well, we see clearly the struggle that ensues when we begin to make contact with what our hearts really hold. And yet we realize it is the only way to be free. God is inviting us to move from our head to our heart. In the heart is where He dwells and where our healing can truly begin.

Tend to Your Vineyard Within

The bride did it, and we can, too. It is so easy to neglect the garden within our own heart that God is cultivating, especially when the Christian value of sacrificially serving others gets out of balance. The problem is, a disconnected heart creates one of the biggest barriers to connecting with ourselves, God, and others in deep and meaningful ways. In John 14:23, one of the last things Jesus tells His disciples is that "My Father will love you so deeply that we will come to you and make you our dwelling place." Where do you think this place of divine-human connection is? Where is this dwelling place?

Your heart!

If we disconnect from our heart, we disconnect from God. My hope is to help you move from a place of intellectualizing your relationship with God into a deep experience of His heart for you, for this is where we encounter the Healer. This means that we have to reconnect with the places within us that we've most neglected. And most often, it is our own emotions.

Spiritual director and author of the book, *Feel*, Anjuli Paschall, makes a bold statement that, "feeling our feelings is biblical."[3] Just read the entire book of Psalms. She goes on to make two important points. One: "Feelings are not my enemy. They are not good or bad; rather they are necessary to have a flourishing relationship with God," and, second, "Feelings are the gravity of intimacy. When followers of God were honest about their feelings, it allowed them to encounter Christ."[4]

Being honest about what we feel creates space for intimacy with God and others and is a necessary component of deep flourishing relationships. Unfortunately, many of us remain stuck at the bottom of the mountain, with our hearts full of longing for more, but entangled in the weeds of our past failures, hurts, fears, and disappointments. Fear and shame are the main reasons we keep our hearts hidden. It can be hard to let our hearts be fully seen. Inevitably, it happens moments after I have been vulnerable with my own heart: the voice of shame tries to surface, telling me I shouldn't have been so honest. I shouldn't have let them know I was struggling and that I don't have it all figured out. Fears about what they are going to think of me surface and I wonder if I've lost their respect.

There is good news. Once we free our minds from having to work so hard not to feel, they can actually experience more of what God intended us to feel: peace, joy, passion, strength, and aliveness. These are our natural states—states that can be experienced more fully when our brains are no longer bogged down by fear. It truly is as the Bible says: "Perfect love drives out fear" (1 John 4:18, NIV) and frees us to experience all God intended for our lives.

Bravely Naming Your Unrecognized Suffering

Often we are living out of a script told by our unhealed stories. I hear them every week from the lips of those I sit alongside within the four walls of my therapy office, these scripts of unrecognized suffering. Most often we tell ourselves, "Oh it isn't that bad, others have it worse, or I shouldn't feel this way." Instead of allowing ourselves to honor the impact of what we've gone through, shame or fear gets piled on top.

It's protective. We minimize, deny or shove away so that we don't have to face the full reality of how much we hurt.

Humans are prone to do this with their emotions. I don't have to tell you that emotions can be complicated. But I do want to point out that what makes them even harder to be with is when they come with warning labels from your past. You could think of them as emotional flashbacks, where your present emotion gets twisted up with an earlier wounding experience creating an even stronger, nonconscious reaction within you. (I use the word "nonconscious" to refer to the material within our mind running under the surface of our awareness.) Then you end up not just having an emotion, but you are also reliving times you had bad experiences with that same emotion in the past.

For example, sadness is an emotion that often gets paired with fear. It is common for people to worry that if they feel their sadness it will never go away, completely overwhelm them, or make them appear weak. Where did these beliefs come from? Somewhere along their timeline, they found themselves alone in the overwhelm of their sadness and had no idea what to do with it, or if they reached out, it wasn't met with the comfort they were seeking. Instead, they got the message, "stop crying, it isn't that bad, or you're just too sensitive."

When we are having these emotional flashbacks, they come with their very own nonconscious defenses or ways we protect ourselves from the hurt of not being validated or seen. We do this by numbing our emotions, shaming ourselves for having emotions, or over intellectualizing our emotions and shutting down all connection with our own body. Anytime we add a negative perception to what is simply the human experience and begin to believe we are wrong, flawed, or weak for having feelings, the very things that were only meant to describe our internal world become so big we learn to fear them, push them away, or shame them back into hiding. We suffer unnecessarily when we are afraid to feel our feelings and we end up becoming enemies with what is going on inside us instead of befriending it.

Many of us have never felt allowed to feel into our emotions fully and discover all that God designed them to do. Emotions help us see the truth about our lives and what matters most to us. Their job is to connect us to others as well as highlight our own needs so that we can take action. But all too often they are deemed the enemy instead.

It's common to grow up conditioned to suppress or disconnect from our authentic emotions. This pattern is often passed down from parents who never learned how to recognize or manage their own emotions in healthy ways. Then when we tried to express what we were feeling and were met with shame, silence, or labels like "too sensitive," we began to neglect our inner world too—learning, often unconsciously, that our feelings were not safe or welcome.

People often say, "I had good parents. I had a great childhood." I said the same. And it is true, I had good parents. But it was decades into my adulthood before I connected the dots. When you grow up in a "good Christian home," sometimes it makes it even harder to see the things you didn't get that you needed. In my case, it wasn't because my parents weren't loving. They were. It was because my parents were running a consuming veterinary practice. My father was an equine reproductive specialist, which meant that whatever we were doing any time, day or night, could change on a dime depending on the phone ringing. Emergency calls were frequent. Foals that needed to be saved. Mares struggling to give birth. Everything in our life revolved around a mare's follicular cycle or other general horse emergencies.

My parents were stressed, distracted and doing the best they could. But the message that began to form in me as a young girl was, "I can't possibly put more stress on them with what is happening within me." There was a sad, lonely, melancholy part of me that had to be shoved away, and the defense that came to my rescue was perfectionism. If I was perfect, no more stress would be added to my parents' plate.

You see, it doesn't take much in childhood to begin to deny our emotional experience and put in place strategies that help us navigate situations we don't yet have the wisdom for. We say in the therapy world that these parts of you that formed when you were young deserve a medal for figuring out how to survive an impossible situation. But now these parts of you need to be updated with a more mature view of life and what is possible.

Understanding Your Emotional Experiences

Let's dive into some neuroscience to better understand why we develop unhealthy, nonconscious patterns that keep us stuck. We'll also explore why failing to acknowledge and validate our emotions can be so painful.

Brains are essentially little prediction machines. They predict what is about to happen and how we need to respond based on our past experiences. Neuroscientist Dan Siegel coined the trendy term "neurons that fire together wire together" to help us understand that the brain pairs things together based on experience as a shortcut.[5] What happens when things begin to pair together is that our brain can get a little rigid and predict that those two things will always be paired together, especially in situations where strong emotions are involved. This can be a great thing when it helps us stay safe from real and present dangers. However, it can also work to our disadvantage when something healthy for us gets unconsciously associated with danger, shame, or fear that don't belong together. To complicate the equation a little further, with any prediction of harm there is also going to be a wired-in defense and protective response. This is a way we adapt to hopefully never feel that similar pain again.

For example, say you reach out to someone in a moment of need and hope to receive comfort. But instead, you feel unseen, invalidated, or misunderstood in some way. Your brain will go to work creating predictions that may sound something like, "If I feel, no one will care, I'll be rejected, I'll be seen as weak." For many of us, we expect negative outcomes around the expression or our emotions and have never connected the dots. If my sadness got paired with an overwhelming sense of being alone and unnoticed, a potential wired in (nonconscious) defense of numbing could form so that I stop feeling at all.

How many adults do you know who don't actually know how they feel?

It's more common than we realize—and there's almost always a painful experience at the root. When, as children, we first reach out for comfort and instead experience rejection or are ignored when we need to be seen, those moments leave an imprint. They become etched into our brains, forming neural pathways that wire together and shape how we respond to emotions and relationships later in life.

Take a moment here to glimpse into the timeline of your past and survey the landscape of your emotional experiences. Growing up were your emotions welcomed or warned away? When you bravely reached out as our emotions are designed to bid us to do, were you unnoticed, or were you told you are just being too sensitive, or that life could be worse? There are so many faulty scripts that get laid in our hearts about emotions that direct us farther and farther away from our own experience and what our hearts hold. This leaves us feeling more alone than ever. Take note of all the negative associations you may have formed over the years about your emotions and about reaching out to others and being seen. When we've been vulnerable and reached out to someone in our pain and it wasn't met in a way we needed, all kinds of things can intertwine that don't belong together.

Being alone in our emotions can be a deeply wounding experience. For many of my clients, having their emotions mishandled by trusted individuals in the past makes it difficult for them to be fully honest about how they feel—even in a safe space like therapy. It can also hinder their ability to truly connect with themselves. If this has been your experience, I understand how frightening it can feel to risk vulnerability again. Often, the safest and most healing place to begin is with God.

Your heart needs a new experience because experience is what changes the brain. The great news is we can change these nonconscious patterns that protected us long ago but now need an update. That update is opening our hearts to new experiences with healthy, healing connections. Nothing makes us feel less alone than being emotionally known. (And I want to recognize at the same time, that if being known in a healthy way has not been your experience, it can feel very unsafe and unsettling to begin to let yourself be seen.)

How then do we allow our hearts to feel safe enough with God that we no longer feel the need to defend or hide ourselves in His presence? We present our whole self open to God so that the false self and faulty scripts within us can be exposed and a rescue mission hand and hand with God can take place.

It reminds me of our discussion about Ezekiel 34 in Chapter 1: God goes in search of us, helping us reconnect with and rediscover the truest self that has been within us all along. As hard as it is, when we face the fears of being seen, we are profoundly undoing our own aloneness. Jesus is so good at this. Healing begins when we have new experiences that contradict what we've always expected.

When we begin to see that emotions are not only safe but also good—that they can be welcomed, fully experienced, and tenderly tended to—something powerful happens. Our brains, which once automatically predicted danger, begin to learn a new story. And little by little, fear loses its grip. One by one, those old patterns of protection begin to gently unravel.

A Practice for Your Heart

Emotions are the conduit to our deepest need: to be seen and known. God designed our emotions to seek acknowledgment. When they have our attention and feel heard, they begin to soften, and the fear centers in our brain quiet down. Emotions were never meant to stay stuck—they were designed to move through us. But that movement only happens when we welcome them and listen.

Do you have at least one person in your life that you feel emotionally known by? If not, let's work on that now. I want to lead you in a practice that will show you how to invite God into the places you need Him most and let Him tend to your heart:

Find a quiet, uninterrupted space and simply begin by finding the rhythm of your breath, in and out. Shift your awareness from your mind to your heart, softening any areas of tension in your body. If it feels comfortable, place your hand over your heart and visualize your breath flowing in and out of this space. Notice the pace of your breath slowing down and deepening ever so slightly. This process of slowing down, entering our heart, and releasing tension opens us to the present moment.

Once you feel more attuned to the tenderness of this moment, reflect on the prompts below. This practice is meant to be a two-way conversation between your heart and God. By the end, you'll have a simple, honest prayer to meditate on each day, allowing God to tend to your needs.

> *"Jesus, I come to You with an honest heart. I need You to know what I am carrying, struggling to shake off, or even afraid to admit to You altogether. So here*

goes. Help me to receive Your compassion as I lay the contents of my heart out before You."

Now, write out what your heart is currently holding.

With your list written, listen for God's tender response. Fill in the following blanks as your heart leads.

_____ (Your Name),

I have seen you struggle with these things and work really hard by:

(Write ways you have tried to solve this on your own)

I know you feel:

(Write out a full list of all the emotions you feel)

And because of the hurt and emotions whirling within, you have been saying to yourself: *(Write out the limiting beliefs, harsh self-criticism or false story you have been believing)*

May I sit with you here in this tender place and encourage you by speaking to your heart what you most need to hear in this moment?

(Write words of compassion that your heart needs to hear the most. You can turn to God's Word or just begin to let the kindest words ever spoken surface within your heart)

Sit here and soak in every ounce of God's compassion, kindness, and love He is expressing toward you in this moment. Don't skip over it or swiftly move onto the next thing. Just sit here and let your heart drink deeply of this moment. Notice God's heart and how it feels for your emotions to be met with love and acceptance rather than shame or judgement.

Your Invitation to Reveal Your Heart

You are invited to the safe space of God's heart where you can heal and come naked before His grace, with no veil between you, hiding nothing. Pour out your hurts and name out loud your worries, as well as your deepest longings and desires. Sit in wonder at how wildly reassuring His love is for you, even when you feel at your worst. Speak this to the Lord and may you hear His response: "Lord, it is You I long for, with no veil between us" (Song of Songs 1:7). Hear him say, "My dearest one, let me tell you how I see you ..." (Song of Songs 1:9).

Second Leg

Reclaim Your Story - Be Reimagined

Now that the foundation of your journey is rooted in His love, there is "inner work" to do to shift how we see ourselves.

The second leg of the journey invites you to respond to His love by reclaiming the truest story God has written for you. This is where we see the bride release the false narrative that once shaped her life, allowing her story to be reimagined through God's eyes.

It is here that the greatest shift begins—in her heart, and in ours. She discovers that what she had been searching for was within her all along, made possible by learning to rest in His love and receiving the truth of how He sees her. This same transformation begins in you as you open your heart to these three invitations:

Capture the Troubling Foxes
Feed on His Word
Say Yes Despite Your Fears

As you respond, your story begins to shift—and the journey toward flourishing takes deeper root.

CHAPTER

5

Invitation 4 – Catch the Troubling Foxes

*"So above all, guard the affections of your heart,
for they affect all that you are. Pay attention
to the welfare of your innermost being, for from there
flows the wellspring of life."*
— Proverbs 4:23

Doubt crept into my heart and quietly took over. Before I even realized it, I was drowning in it. I had been so certain this time would be different. Four years ago, I began dreaming about—and writing—the very book you are now holding. I had joined a well-known Christian author's bootcamp, investing significant time, money, and hope into the process. Looking back now, I can see how desperation had seeped into my soul because

I had convinced myself that this was my last chance. Afterall, my previous self-published book had completely failed to meet all my lofty expectations and this time I was sure God was up to something. To me, it was the perfect opportunity to bring the message of healing God had placed in my heart out into the world.

But in the end, all my hopes were crushed by another "no." It was confusing and heartbreaking. Even now, as I recall it, I feel tears forming in the corners of my eyes. To be honest, I didn't want to write about this part of my story and had excluded it in my first draft. It made me feel ashamed, as if there must have been something about me that didn't measure up because He chose not to open the door. The deeper danger of this insidious doubt that surfaced within me was that it made me pull away and believe that God didn't have my back. I distanced myself from Him and others which only increased my feelings of aloneness. And I stopped writing this book for four years. These are the things that are difficult to confront in our stories and painful to examine, yet they are vitally necessary to identify if we want to grow beyond our fears and doubts.

In moments of doubt, defenses form. They go hand in hand. This chapter is a deep dive into understanding the pattern of doubt and defense within you. That means there are things you may have to look at that you have long avoided or never even realized were connected in the first place. Within this chapter, we will identify the foxes of compromise, comparison, self-doubt, and self-defense. In just a few chapters, we will learn how to say yes to our truest self despite our doubts and fears with brave and bold action steps. For now, we must get really certain about how and when these pesky thieves sneak into our thought life.

Out of Nowhere They Appear

My heart sinks here for the bride as I reflect on this part of her journey, maybe because it just feels all too familiar to my experience. Here we get a glimpse into the battle we all will face as believers. You see, the bride has been practicing a new way of being. She has been spending time at rest in God's love, revealing her heart, and listening for His response. She has been learning a new dimension of His heart and has begun to soak in the words that He has spoken over her. Her heart is gradually shifting, changing, and opening to a new perspective as He diligently reveals what He has planted within her and her destiny.

Then, what seemed like out of nowhere, *they* appeared—those old pesky doubts and limiting beliefs. They seek to keep her from flourishing and connecting with God's heart. They attempt to separate her from what is rightfully hers. God tells her to "Arise, my dearest. Hurry, my darling. Come away with me! I have come as you have asked to draw you to my heart and lead you out. ... Can you not discern this new day of destiny breaking forth around you? The early signs of my purposes and plans are bursting forth" (Song of Songs 2:10 and 13). And then the Bridegroom says, "You must catch the troubling foxes, those sly little foxes that hinder our relationship. For they raid our budding vineyard of love to ruin what I've planted within you. Will you catch them and remove them for me? We will do it together" (Song of Songs 2:15).

How does the bride respond to His request for her to go higher with Him and recognize the sly hindrances that try to keep her from doing so? Let's see as I take the liberty of paraphrasing verses 16 and 17. She begins by expressing her belief in the fact that He loves her, and she has everything she needs in Him. Then she throws out an emphatic, "But my fears and doubts are screaming loudly, I don't think I can do it. I don't think I have what it takes. You must go on without me!"

You see why my heart sinks? He is calling her higher into her destiny, promising to be with her, and then doubts surface and the uncertainty paralyzes her. Can you see yourself here? In your own journey with God, have you found yourself saying, "I just can't—I don't have what it takes"?

As believers, our journey will always come with opposition. This is something we must be aware of and vigilant about because every great love story has a villain. There is a reason Peter writes about it in 1 Peter 5:8-9. He warns us to "Be well balanced and always alert, because your enemy, the devil, roams around incessantly, like a roaring lion looking for its prey to devour. Take a decisive stand against him and resist his every attack with strong, vigorous faith."

I love Peter. I can really identify with him. He was passionate and fiery, yet had times when he was thrown off track by doubt and fear. I've found myself doing the same. I'm moving forward full of hope and energy, pursuing something with all my heart, then out of nowhere, doubt hits me and stops me dead in my tracks. I'm blindsided by thoughts like, "Who am I to do this? What am I doing? Maybe God didn't call me to this. Maybe my motivation is all wrong." I end up feeling completely beaten down, ready to run and hide. How does it happen so quickly?

This is why Peter was set on warning believers of the real enemy who's always lurking, ready to devour us. He knew what it was like firsthand. He'd experienced the devastation of doubt's influence. He walked with Jesus, knew Him intimately, and when everything he trusted was shaken—strong, fierce Peter was overcome with doubt. We know the story: when confronted about his connection to Jesus, Peter denied Him three times. I can easily judge and question how it happened, yet it occurs within our hearts every day to some degree.

We have a real enemy of our souls, and his goal isn't just to intimidate or shake us up a little. He wants to *kill, steal, and destroy* what is truest about us. It's important to get acquainted with and know how to resist our own "troubling foxes"—the doubts and fears that creep in and derail us when we least expect it.

What we won't do is give the enemy more power than he deserves, but we are seeking to be aware and vigilant of how slyly he operates. I will tell you this: he is not about to become quiet. He will keep picking away at the wounds, doubts, and places he knows will discourage you. Yet the more we know, the greater our chances of resisting his advances.

There is a reason this journey is hard, and it is because your healing and freedom are opposed. Yet we are given a promise in John 10:10 that Christ came so that we can have life and live more abundantly. God's promise is to restore you so that you can live your authentic story, your undisputed origin story, and live it to the fullest. So, what then are these sly little foxes and how do we start to recognize when they are sneaking in to steal, kill, and destroy what God is planting within us?

Just How Much Harm Could One Little Old Fox Do?

Jesus used metaphors and stories to teach deeper principles of the heart, and we see this powerfully illustrated in the Song of Songs. Though the Bible doesn't mention foxes frequently, when they do appear, they carry deep implications for reflection. Foxes are most notably symbols of opposition and cunning trickery. These small creatures are destructive forces known to be detrimental to agriculture (to growth). When you think about the Bible's mention of wolves, most of us know to be wary. Foxes, however, are more subtle and harder to detect. They may even appear cute, but their deceitful, deceptive nature makes them a more insidious threat.

In the Songs, foxes represent a metaphorical warning. They urge us to see that small, seemingly insignificant issues we don't confront can harm or destroy something more significant being cultivated within us—like the beauty planted within our hearts. These small disturbances, though often overlooked, can disrupt our spiritual and relational well-being. Vigilance is required to maintain connection with God.

Galatians 5:7-9 (NIV) provides another insightful metaphor: "You were running a good race. Who cut in on you to keep you from obeying the truth? That kind of persuasion does not come from the one who calls you. 'A little yeast works through the whole batch of dough.'" Verse ten goes on to say, "I am confident in the Lord that you will take no other view. The one who is throwing you into confusion, whoever that may be, will have to pay the penalty" (Galatians 5:10, NIV). The Passion Translation is more direct as it asks: "Don't you know that when you allow even a little lie into your heart, it can permeate your entire belief system?" (Galatians 5:9, TPT). It's surprising how easily it can happen.

Troubling foxes or beliefs that form within us are like the yeast that spreads through the whole loaf of bread. Doubt by its very nature is demoralizing, distracting, and weakens our spirit and faith.

Unfortunately, many people live trapped in the status quo and just like the bride, they stay at the bottom of the mountain. They send God away, convinced by doubt that they don't have what it takes. This leads us into the first type of troubling fox we need to identify.

Foxes of Compromise

Compromise happens when we begin to accept less than what we were made for. The Bridegroom is trying to awaken the bride to her destiny, to her divine mission, when He says, "Can you not discern this new day of destiny breaking forth around you? The early signs of my purposes and plans are bursting forth" (Song of Songs 2:13). The foxes of compromise represent earthly security. We compromise divine mission at times for earthly comfort. Living the life God has called us to will mean sacrifice. It will cost us something. It is easy to disregard what Jesus meant when He said, "Take up your cross." When the trek up the mountain gets hard, we often settle for lower standards and choose to remain in the status quo.

When we compromise, the behavior that often follows is complaining or even blaming others or our circumstances because we feel shame for shying away from or watering down who we know in our hearts we are meant to be. I hate to admit that at times I am the queen of complaining. This sly little troubling fox sneaks into my thoughts quickly and swiftly before I even know what is coming out of my mouth. Most of the time, our complaining represents a legitimate need or desire, yet it is steeped in self-effort and lacks any semblance of surrendered trust.

With compromise and complaining, we end up letting the world and circumstances diminish our awareness of God's intention for our lives. In what ways have you possibly lowered your standards to remain comfortable and play it safe, thus minimizing the calling on your life? Have you found yourself getting lost in complaining about the circumstances surrounding you, or angry and blaming others for getting in your way? In the end, it is a troubling fox, slyly sneaking in to rob, kill, and destroy.

Foxes of Comparison

The little girl in me and the little girl in you just wants to matter and to be noticed. For women especially, I do think this mind battle of comparison is fierce. I find that when I compare myself with other women leaders, it is easy for me to feel despair. We live in a digital world that's full of opportunities for toxic comparison. It's a relentless assault on a woman's heart.

Every woman we see out there doing what we aspire to do can feed the narrative of our own inadequacy. When I read Galatians 5:26, it hit me in the gut. Paul writes, "So may we never be arrogant, or look down on another, for each of us is an original. We must forsake all jealousy that diminishes the value of others." Ouch, that hurts. I don't want to be the woman who diminishes the value of someone else! We are all originals, and when I find myself jealous of another woman who is out there doing what I want to be doing, I am diminishing her value. As you sit here in this reflective moment, ask yourself, how has comparing myself to other women diminished both my value and theirs?

Foxes of Self-Doubt

I have yet to meet a woman who doesn't struggle with some version of self-doubt or fear of inadequacy—wondering if she's enough or if she's capable. These sly, seemingly little foxes show up for me in thoughts like: "I can't, I don't have what it takes, I'm not a good business woman, etc," which leads to seemingly small compromises. I didn't send the email. I didn't sign up for the women's speaker list. I choose not to reach out. These inactions add up. I'm sure I've avoided doing more than I realize.

Have you found yourself there too? You know those moments in your life where God is nudging you to do something, and you convince yourself that you just can't or that you will mess it all up. It is an agonizing wrestling match within isn't it?

It shows up for me most often when I have felt like my efforts haven't been rewarded or noticed. I can easily find myself saying, *"I guess I am just not good enough."* Then my self-critical voice takes over and down into a dark place I go.

One of the first things I found the Lord emphasizing when studying the Song of Song journey was a need to stop beating myself up. I realized being self-critical is the easiest way for the enemy of our souls to enter in and begin to tear up what God has been planting in us. Why? Because we are aligning with the wrong voice. And if we don't confront our self-critical voice and learn to silence it, there is no way to continue up the mountain into our most flourishing life.

Our self-critical voice can take the form of overthinking, ruminating about what we should've, could've done differently, and then we question everything. Ultimately, I think it comes down to the fact that we like to feel in control. But life just doesn't offer us that certainty, and when we find ourselves stuck in the mental state of uncertainty, self-doubt grows feverishly. What self-doubt or critical voice prevents you from recognizing all that is already within you? What keeps you from reaching out or taking steps toward something you know God is asking you to bravely do?

Foxes of Self-defense

This is the troubling fox I warned you about at the beginning of the chapter—the one we most want to avoid dealing with. The troubling fox of self-defense represents our survival instincts. Because these instincts often operate nonconsciously—automatically, beneath our conscious awareness—we need to focus intentionally on this particular belief. First, we'll explore how these troubling foxes of self-defense are formed.

A hurt animal tucked in a corner will instinctively defend itself. When we are hurt or threatened, we do the same. So, it makes sense then that these troubling foxes form as a defense against our wounds. And because we have both the benefit and detriment at times of being the only mammal with the most advanced neocortex "thinking brain," our wounding moments also come with wounding messages. They often sound something like: *"It's not okay to be me,"* *"There must be something wrong with me,"* or *"It's all my fault."*

Keep in mind these defenses form automatically when we experience any moment of threat in our nervous system whether psychological, say through a moment of rejection, or physically. The intention of a defense is to protect us from further wounding, rejection, or hurt. What ends up happening within us often follows this progression: wounds create wounding messages or limiting beliefs, then wounding messages naturally create defenses.

We all have these patterns to varying degrees. These defenses have been around longer than we might realize. I work with individuals all the time who feel stuck in patterns they don't understand and wish they didn't feel compelled to do. Some patterns are clear to them, but they still don't understand why they do them, while others they remain unaware of. Since these defenses most often are formed within us when we are young, discovering them sometimes requires the tender and compassionate presence of another to help uncover them.

This process is illustrated in the bride's story. In Chapter 3 of the *Songs*, we see a pivotal moment in her journey. She had just sent the Bridegroom away up the mountain, overwhelmed by her fears and doubts. Her thoughts might have been something like, "I can't do this. I don't have what it takes." Soon, however, she regrets her decision. She sets out to find Him, and when she does, she says, "I encountered him. I found the one I adore! I caught him and fastened myself to him, refusing to be feeble in my heart again. Now I'll bring him back to the temple within where I was given new birth—into my innermost parts, the place of my conceiving" (Song of Songs 3:4).

She returns to her past with Him and takes an honest look at her family of origin to uncover where her defenses first formed. Something within her knew this was a step that she could not skip if she wanted to be free.

The bride's story shows us that to move forward, we must first go back. It seems counterintuitive, I know, but there is a story we must honor. We have to go back and honor the story of the little girl, the teenager, even the young adult inside of us. The impact of our wounding moments must be acknowledged. I've watched my clients struggle with this, as they fear they are "blaming" others. But what they are actually doing is finally honoring their story and naming the impact of the painful moments they endured with tenderness instead of shame. It is a necessity if we want to flourish and live out our most authentic story. Pastor Pete Scazzero explains this so beautifully when he says, "The work of growing in Christ does not mean we don't go back to the past as we press ahead to what God has for us. It actually demands we go back in order to break free from unhealthy and destructive patterns that prevent us from loving ourselves, and others as God designed."[1]

Like the bride, we must bravely look back, holding Jesus' hand, and identify the foxes of self-defense that have taken root within us. If we don't, they will prevent us from seeing the fruit of what God is planting in us. The bride's decision to send Him away, and her subsequent regret, drove her to discover what was underneath her actions. She knew that to move forward, she had to revisit the roots of these beliefs and sever their hold over her. We must do the same.

Most of the templates our brains form about who we are and how the world works are created in the first five years of our lives. Dr. Bruce Perry, a renowned child psychiatrist, explains in his book, *What Happened to You?* how the past shapes our current functioning: "Moment by moment in early life, our developing brain sorts and stores our personal experiences, making our personal 'codebook' that helps us interpret the world. Each of us creates a unique worldview shaped by our life's experience .... The experiences in the first years of life are disproportionately powerful in shaping how our brain organizes."[2]

We often say, "The past is the past. I've dealt with it already." But more often than not, this is a defense we've built around our hearts. And it becomes a troubling fox that must be caught. Have you ever stopped to consider how your heart was handled growing up and how it shaped you into the person you are today? Jesus calls to us, saying, "You have to let me get to that, dear one." Jesus came to restore us, and He declares this mission clearly in Isaiah 61:1, "The mighty Spirit of Lord Yahweh is wrapped around me because Yahweh has anointed me, ... he sent me to heal the wounds of the brokenhearted, to tell captives, 'You are free,' and to tell prisoners, 'Be free from your darkness.'"

Our True Selves Need Rescued

We need to go on a rescue mission and rediscover our truest self. Here is where we begin the process of allowing God to help us reimagine our story. The truest self within us has been sequestered away, so we invite God in to help us go search for her. We have a certainty that as we travel this harrowing path of naming our wounding moments and the defenses that have resulted, God's goodness and love are pursuing us all the way (Psalm 23:6). He came to restore and free us (Isaiah 61) and promises to search for us even if no one else has (Ezekiel 34).

Shame, however, has a different plan. It wants us to remain hidden. It is scary to be seen because our hearts may not have always been handled gently, but this rescue mission is vital. At the end, we get to see face to face the truest part of us that contains the seeds of what God planted within us from the very beginning. This is the part of us that we thought we had to hide because it wasn't okay to be her, or we weren't worthy of being her. In order to free her, there are parts of us that hold messages and wounding moments that now need to be turned to with eyes of compassion so that they can heal.

I encourage my clients with the truth that within them is their core truest self—the self that God uniquely crafted, created, and shaped. If I were sitting in front of you right now, I would tell you that what is truest about you is found where God dwells—in the deepest part of you. Nothing you have experienced in life can take your truest self away or damage her. The only thing painful life experiences can do is cover her up with weeds that keep her from growing and being seen. The truth is she is whole, balanced, and complete within you, and is longing to be rediscovered. When we partner with God in this space within us, that is where healing can happen.

Let's begin to name the troubling foxes that are stifling your truest self and trying to keep her hidden within your heart. This will shed light on the defenses that have formed as a solution to the wounding moments you experienced.

Take a moment to grab a piece of paper. It is important to write it down so you can see what is whirling in your heart and mind more clearly. This will be the beginning of reimaging your story through God's eyes. But first we need to know what limiting beliefs need to be reimagined.

This can be a triggering process as strong emotions will most likely begin to rise to the surface. Read through the directions below and note within your own nervous system, "Does this feel right for me to do at this time, or to do on my own?" Trust your instincts and be extra kind to yourself as we dive into what could be sensitive areas within you.

First, in the center of a blank page I want you to draw a circle. Write the words, "My true core self, my truest self, my God designed self"—whatever words most resonate with you. Now, I want you to take a moment to envision what is truest about you and get a really good look at her. What makes you feel most alive when you experience it? What act, service, characteristic or way of being in the world makes you say, "Yes, this is who I am. This feels most true about who I want to be! This is why I am here on this earth." Describe her in depth and write all the characteristics that bubble up within that circle.

Next you will draw another circle around your true self. Within this circle you will write a simple word or phrase (no details needed) that helps you acknowledge the wounding moments you experienced and the negative messages you then internalized. Ask yourself, "What paralyzing messages have my wounded moments created? What story did I begin to believe that shaped how I see myself, the world, others, and God?" These are the moments when shame, pain, or an unmet need entered your story. These occur in all of our lives. Many of my clients start to struggle here, dismissing, denying, or minimizing their pain with words like, "Oh it wasn't that bad, others had it worse." May I gently pause here, and invite you to turn toward your own heart—just as you would a beloved friend—and see what it's holding through eyes of compassion, not judgment.

What wounds from when you were little up until today does your heart hold? Keep in mind, when painful experiences happen to us when we are young and egocentric (because our brains haven't fully developed), we are more likely to internalize a message of shame that says, *"It is all my fault, or something must be wrong with, defective or bad about me."*

It is the defenses shaped by these wounding moments and messages that we will bring awareness to next. Now you will draw an even wider circle around the wound and wounding messages you identified and name the ways you responded to those wounds and messages (your self-defenses or protective parts). These are autonomic ways of being that when created were intended to protect you from ever feeling that same pain, rejection, shame again with the hopes of instead receiving love, acceptance, and approval.

I'll illustrate this process with an example from my own life (figure 1). When I think about my truest self, these are words I would write in the center circle: compassionate, empathetic, creative, passionate, at ease, curious, hope-filled, faithful, steadfast, wholehearted, a writer of words that heal the soul, a healer, confident, wanted, fun, relaxed, balanced, complete, chosen, loved, and one who reveals God's goodness and heart to the world. Those feel good in my soul. They resonate deeply with who I am, what makes me come alive and describe how I want to live this one life I have.

In the next circle, I identify my wounds and wounded messages and how shame, pain and unmet needs entered my story causing me to disconnect from my truest self. I identify my wounding moments as, rejected by others, growing up alone in my emotions, fighting in my home. Then I write the corresponding wounding messages my wounding moments created: I am weird and different, my emotions are too big for me and others and I have to be perfect so no one else hurts or gets too stressed. The most common beliefs identified by clients over the years are: I am not enough, I'm too much, I am not safe, I can't trust anyone, I am worthless, I am all alone, no one cares, or I am abandoned. As you seek to name the messages created in your own heart you will hear subtle nuances that were created through your specific experiences. The "I am not enough" belief might be more like "I am a disappointment" if that is how you always felt in the presence of one of your caregivers who was raising your tender heart.

The next circle represents my automatic defenses that came to my rescue. The solutions that formed, primarily when I was young, with the goal of protecting me from further hurt, shame, or rejection. Within this circle I write: self-reliance, perfectionism, extreme self-criticism, workaholism, and seeking others' approval for validation of worth. My clients have written things like: depression, panic, hopelessness, restricting eating, binging, pushing people away, excessive caregiving, numbing emotions, over-analyzing, people-pleasing, isolating, self-medicating. The list of ways we protect ourselves can go on and on.

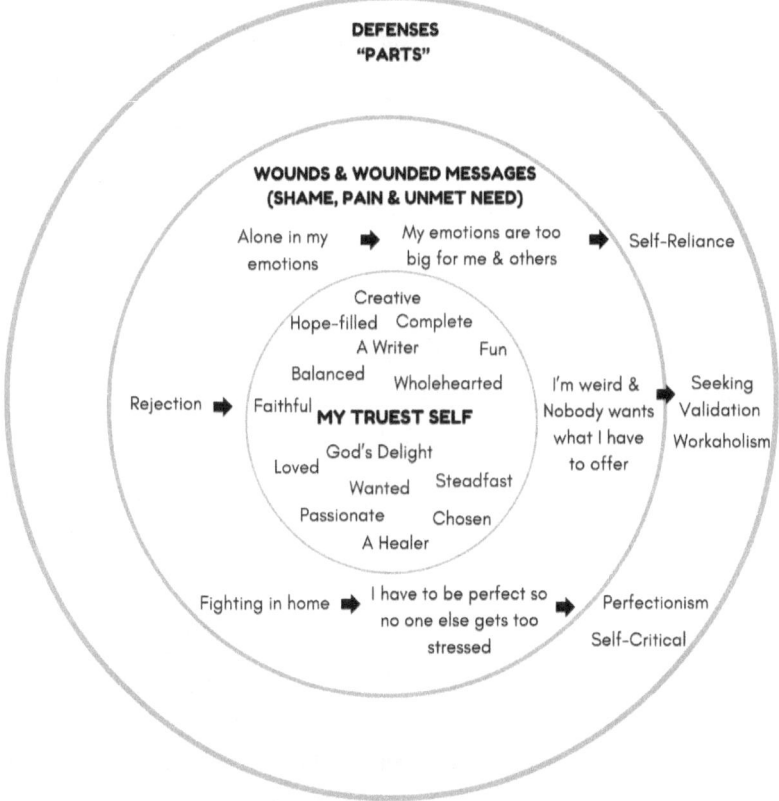

Figure 1

The good news is we don't stop here. In the next few chapters, we seek to feed on the truth that frees us and find new ways of being in the world that help us reconnect with our truest selves, and live out the life God designed for us all along! I know this part of the journey can be heavy. The hope we have is God does not leave us here. There is healing on the way.

I do also want to mention that if the wounded moments feel too much to bear or work through alone, that makes complete sense. Please reach out to a therapist who specializes in trauma and get the support you deserve. Healing isn't meant to be done alone. We always get the best results when our hearts can be tenderly witnessed by another. I would also encourage you to remember that this process takes time and to purposefully slow down as you observe yourself and what your heart holds. Remember most of these patterns were formed when you were young and require careful, compassionate eyes to discover them.

Troubling Fox Self-Inventory

As we end this chapter let's remember one of the first priorities we have while endeavoring to live a flourishing life, which is to grow in self-awareness. Becoming more aware of the voice of your troubling foxes and how and when they creep in will help you overcome them. This is important because we know that anytime we start to get a glimpse of what God is growing in us the enemy sends his troubling foxes to snatch it up and stop our growth. It is important that we take a moment to do a little self-inventory and think about the troubling foxes we've been looking at. Reflect on these questions to see which troubling foxes most hinder your progress and which one (or two) you most need to name and invite Jesus in to help you overcome them:

- Have you compromised the longings within your heart by minimizing, discrediting, or dismissing a dream because the cost felt too high?

- Are there earthly comforts you have been seeking that have kept you in the space of "status quo" because it just seems easier?

- Have there been moments in your life where you felt you were less than, not as good as, or not as worthy as other women pursuing what you feel called to do?

- Have you let go of a promise from the Lord because of one too many disappointments, the wait has felt too long, or you felt forgotten?

- Have you taken steps of faith only to shrink back and sink into obscurity because self-doubt told you that you are inadequate or don't have what it takes?

- Have you felt tossed about by doubt that constantly makes you feel unsettled and uncertain about what God has called you to do?

- Have unhealed wounds from your past kept you from moving forward?

- Have wounded messages driven by inner shame, pain, or an unmet need convinced you that somehow it isn't okay to be you?

Which troubling foxes are most troubling you: compromise, comparison, self-doubt or self-defense?

My friend, foxes are everywhere. Opposition will always come against what is truest about us. I don't like it, but it makes sense.

One of the greatest ways the enemy of our soul worms his way into our thought life and paralyzes us is through doubt. From the very beginning in the garden, his tactic hasn't changed—because he knows it works. He leads us to doubt what God has said, and to question whether we have enough or are enough with what we've already been given.

As I end this chapter, experience these words as if God was speaking them from His heart directly to yours. May they soak in and change you from the inside out. Giving you courage, hope and a vision for the path ahead that is all your own! Hear Him say:

Oh, my dear lovely one, I need you to know that an onslaught of doubt has been launched against your heart for what it contains are seeds that change the world and atmospheres around you. If you only knew what I've placed within you. If you could only see in this moment and embrace it. Even a sliver of it will do. My dear, it is so mighty what I've designed you with. You have only been listening to one side of the story, now I need you to listen to mine. Here in this place is a major transition, a crossroad that is so vital to the path that I have for you; where you lay down the story that has been holding you back and grab ahold of what I have for you in this moment. I need you to know that I've written a song for you, a song only your soul can sing. Only you have the lyrics. I've written them in gold upon your soul and I've sealed them with my love. No one and nothing can ever separate you from the truest, deepest, loveliest you that is within your soul. She is in you, my dear. You've been listening to the wrong song. This world cannot rob you of the song I've placed in you, but it can do everything possible to distort the sound of it by distracting you, discouraging you and making you doubt what I've placed within you. Will you listen to my heart being sung over you right now? Be still and listen deeply to this sweet melody. It is the sound of the truest you resonating and reverberating all throughout your being. She is within you, my dear, and she is so lovely, so adorned with beauty. She has a message to share, a love to express, a unique way of being in my world that is all her own and is absolutely 100% irreplaceable by anyone else. My dear, you are it! Only you can share this song. I need you to believe in what I have placed within you. Don't for a second let your heart say it doesn't matter, it isn't enough, or that another song is better. I need you to arise and awaken to the destiny I have for you! May you never forget your voice again. I am with you. I have taken you by the hand. You are mine! I will never let go. Let's do this together, forever together!

Your Invitation to Catch the Troubling Foxes

You are invited to boldly confront the voice of doubt that surfaces within you and identify the ways it makes you compromise and shrink back your faith, compare and not feel enough, doubt your abilities or shame you into obscurity. Hear Him ask you, "You must catch the troubling foxes, those sly little foxes that hinder our relationship. For they raid our budding vineyard of love to ruin what

I've planted within you. Will you catch them and remove them for me? We will do it together" (Song of Songs 2:15).

CHAPTER

6

Invitation 5 –
Feed on His Word

*"The primary purpose of God giving us Scripture is that we
would know who we are in His Sight."*
- Graham Cooke

One morning, not too long ago, I sat in my dimly lit corner
nook seeking God's direction. I was feeling overwhelmed
and anxious. Distractions were constant and clarity was
hard to find. A thought had been rolling around in my mind that
was odd for me. I'd always firmly believed in a deep sense of personal
purpose and that my life here has meaning. It is a reality that has
given me peace over the years, but suddenly, that peace left, and I
found myself questioning my existence in a way I hadn't before. I
was in a midlife funk, questioning, *"Have I really accomplished
anything?"*

As I reflected, I realized that questioning my purpose surfaced from trying to decide what to let go of. Should I keep my full-time job and risk my well-being or should I jump into a part-time position and let go of my financial security and status? On one hand, giving up my full-time job meant I was leaving a toxic work environment behind, and on the other, it meant I was jumping into complete financial insecurity and letting go of a sense of accomplishment I had worked so hard to achieve. As the months passed, I began to realize how much my identity (no matter how many years I'd worked on it) depended on what I could accomplish—on recognition, on a role, and the level I had achieved in my career.

As I sat in my chair and came clean with Jesus about all of it, something began to stir and rise up within me. I heard myself say, "God is an intentional designer. It is just not who He is to design someone without purpose. It is not His nature." His Word that I had fed on over and over through the years began to bubble up within me and encourage me. I recalled Genesis and how at the very beginning, He created me in His image. How could someone created in His image not have purpose?

Then suddenly, one of my all-time favorite verses came to mind. Ephesians 2:10 says, "We have become his poetry, a re-created people that will fulfill the destiny he has given each of us, for we are joined to Jesus, the Anointed One. Even before we were born, God planned in advance our destiny and the good works we would do to fulfill it!" And then how could I forget Ephesian 1:11: "Before we were even born, he gave us our destiny, that we would fulfill the plan of God who always accomplishes every purpose and plan in his heart." My heart began to beat with confidence as I thought about God thinking of me and then designing me—breathing life into me.

I found myself saying, "Come on, Josie, does that sound like your life doesn't have purpose just because you are no longer in this role?"

It reminds me of the Psalmist's words in Psalm 42:11: "So I say to my soul, 'Don't be discouraged. Don't be disturbed. For I know my God will break through for me.' Then I'll have plenty of reasons to praise him all over again. Yes, he is my saving grace!" This verse beautifully illustrates the importance of being aware of the troubling foxes and defenses we began identifying in the last chapter—so we can make space for truth, reimagine our story, and align our hearts with what God says about us.

Let God Reimagine Your Story

In the last chapter, we started to see where our true story was overtaken by wounding moments and wounding messages that naturally created defenses. These defenses came to our rescue in moments of emotional overwhelm, loneliness, or pain and formed their own protective net around our hearts. As you recall, our defenses become symptoms of the original wounding.

Often, in the mental health field, we try to manage the symptoms (people pleasing, depression, panic, social withdrawal, substance abuse) and fail to get to the root wound that created the need for the defense in the first place. Without healing the wound, the defense, or symptom will always be needed. I believe in focusing on and solving the issue at its root rather than just teaching my clients skills to manage the symptoms that their wounds created. Understanding why this pattern or defense feels necessary can lead us to the underlying wound and the hurtful message that needs healing.

Once we recognize the web we are stuck in, we can free ourselves from its grip. Next, we need to invite God into our wounded places so He can help us reimage our story. One way this is accomplished is through feeding on His Word. When we stumble across a truth that logically makes sense, but our hearts reject it, this points to where we must place our focus. This will require allowing our hearts to have a new experience, one that contradicts the original wounding message.

When we slow down and intentionally pay attention we can develop greater self-awareness and bring nonconscious material into conscious awareness. One way we do this is by noticing our responses in the moment. Let me ask you this. As soon as you feel an emotion, let's say sadness, what is the immediate reaction within you? Do you feel your chest tighten? Is there a message that surfaces that makes you feel somehow it isn't okay to be sad? Maybe you fear that feeling sadness will lead to it overwhelming and flooding you, or that you will forever be stuck there.

As another example, let's consider the belief rooted in the wounded message "I don't deserve love." Maybe the original wound that created this message was born in a home where the child's parents were workaholics and believed in extreme stoicism. There were no hugs, no moments of tender I love you's. They never attended a school function or smiled with delight over a drawing brought home. Being unnoticed became the norm. The heart must guard itself in unsafe spaces such as this. So many defenses can form, but we will say in this scenario, a people-pleaser was created to live out the story of unlovability. The wounding message that drives their actions is, "I am only lovable if I give, do, please, and appease". A constant cycle of dishonoring their voice, needs, wants begins in a desperate attempt to just be seen, loved, and accepted if only for a moment. This leads one down a life-long path of an inability to receive love just for being who they are.

Acknowledgement is where healing can *begin*. I emphasize *begin* because it is now a journey of undoing the old wounding message to embrace a new story in its place. The story of love, and our own lovability, begins to take shape in the heart that opens to new experiences with love—a love that once was seen as underserved, a love that surprisingly and shockingly unconditionally accepts them just for who they are, a love that wants to hear their voice, honor their opinion, and desires to meet their needs. At first, it may not feel real—but over time, experience after experience begins to contradict the original wounding messages, gently opening the heart to healing and the possibility of believing in one's own lovability.

Taking Back Ground

Why is all this discovery and uncovering work necessary from a spiritual perspective? Pastor Bill Johnson masterfully points out what is required if what we seek is to mature and grow further in our walk with God. He says, "Thinking incorrectly not only empowers the enemy, it gives him a safe place to hide." And he further explains that "strongholds are whatever people trust in other than God."[2]

Our defenses become strongholds. They are the beliefs and method of self-protection that have formed within us that we have unknowingly come to trust in more than God's truth. They provide a hiding place for the enemy to push out God's truth from our hearts. 2 Corinthians 10: 3-5 says:

> For though we live in the world, we do not wage
> war as the world does. The weapons we fight with

are not the weapons of the world. On the contrary, they have divine power to demolish strongholds. We demolish arguments and every pretension that sets itself up against the knowledge of God, and we take captive every thought to make it obedient to Christ. (NIV)

I am a firm believer in the transforming power of God's Word. It has completely changed my life. And yet, people often don't realize why reading more Scripture by itself sometimes doesn't seem to work. If we are unaware of the web we are caught in and the thoughts that need to be captured and thrown down, they will remain in our hearts, resisting the truth and revelation God's Word is providing. It is essential to recognize and articulate the interconnected web that binds our hearts. Most often, the wounding messages from our past experiences create a cavernous hiding place for the enemy to silence the voice of truth within us.

The reality is that we can't capture and throw down what we don't realize exists within our hearts and minds. Which is why I am suggesting merging mental health principles, (by which I am referring to self-reflection and growing in self-awareness) with the spiritual practice of reading Scripture. One thing I asked of the Lord in writing this book was to allow me to personally experience every invitation. I wasn't going to ask you to go anywhere I had not already been, and since the thought that I have no purpose kept surfacing over and over, it became the place I dug a little deeper. I found my heart was holding a wounding message yet to be discovered.

I first tuned into the anxiety I had been feeling and mentioned in the beginning of this chapter. I sat with the sensation in my chest.

I welcomed it. I knew I needed to understand what message my anxiety was trying to show me and reveal the "wounding message" that was causing me to feel discouraged and without purpose. Turns out there was more to the story.

As I looked deeper, I found that it was an old familiar fear of inadequacy and failure that carried with it a distrust in God. I scanned the timeline of my life and saw me, in my early thirties. My head was hanging heavy beneath my shoulders and my heart was deadened. This was one of the hardest parts of my story. I had just lost my dad suddenly and unexpectedly, which subsequently led to losing the ministry we had worked so hard to build for over a decade. This part of me felt rage.

As I sat with the rage within me, I felt a physical, guttural punch. It was the same gut-wrenching grief I experienced when sitting in my father's truck, moments after coming home from the hospital the night he died. My head was pressed against his steering wheel trying to make sense of what had happened. I was replaying the image of the doctor's face as he exited my father's hospital room and hearing his muffled words, "I am sorry, he didn't make it."

It was here, as I visually recalled this moment, that the dots began connecting. I couldn't believe I was saying it, and yet it just rolled off my tongue: "You take everything away, God." This belief that formed about God in the middle of my grief had been unspoken and slyly sitting in my heart for years. I felt like everything I had worked for just slipped through my hands and I couldn't understand why.

Over a decade had passed since my father died, and I was just now discovering that this hardened part of my heart had formed. The healing journey is life-long. It isn't a checklist, or a destination point you arrive at. It is a process, often with many layers. I had been a therapist walking people through their wounding moments (and doing my own work as well) for twenty years by this point. And here I found myself shocked, in disbelief, and blind to how the pain of loss had closed off my heart.

You see, I was a daddy's girl. He saw my heart in a way few others ever could. He had this beautiful way of reflecting the good in me and reminding me of who I was when I forgot. I never once questioned his love. Losing that kind of steady, affirming presence so suddenly was a crushing gift to lose. And under the weight of that loss, I floundered. The grief didn't just break my heart; it clouded my sense of identity, security, and belonging. Looking from the outside, you would never have known. In fact, I had even convinced myself I was fine. But the truth was, part of my heart had hardened when my dad died, and twelve years later, it hadn't come back to life. Surprisingly, you can convince yourself that you're doing well for much longer than one might expect.

God began to gently pull back these layers of pain that had settled within me to reveal where I most needed my story to be reimagined through His truth. He was helping me see what needed to be captured and where I had created a hiding place for the enemy to sneak in his lies. I began by looking at why I was suddenly resisting believing that I had a purpose. The pain of losing my dad and then the ministry I loved felt unbearable at times. The internal message created from that wound was, "I mess everything up; no wonder you haven't blessed me with more, Lord."

Thoughts like that need defending. So, a fog came over my mind. It shut me down. Vision and purpose were nowhere to be found in the denseness of it surrounding me. The brain fog was an attempt to protect me from yet another loss that this part of me feared would destroy me completely. I started to see how I had been running from my truest self ever since. My attempts at jobs, roles, and recognition created a safe distance from the ministry God had placed on my heart to lead and the story I was really made for. It paralyzed me at times, and quite frankly, I was tired of it.

Interestingly, as I peered back into the vision of my thirty-something self, I started to see that within her my heart was still beating. I was reminded of who I was before life tried to deaden this part of me. I was reminded that no matter what life had stolen or how much it hurt, the truest passion within me was still alive. I was reminded of what I loved and had forgotten. His truth I had been feeding on over the years shined through the fog and reminded me that God is an intentional designer and always has been. It turns out no matter what life brings, this truest part of me and the truest part of you can never be taken away.

We see this struggle within the bride when her troubling foxes won the last round. The Bridegroom warned her about them, but she did not realize what they were and how deeply they were planted within her heart. They caused her to send him away. The doubt and the fears were so loud and convincing. Once she saw the mountain before her, she felt small and insignificant. But as soon as He turned to walk up the mountain without her, she regretted her decision. It was in the pain of this reality that she found Him and took Him back to her past. She was determined to identify what troubling foxes had formed in her and why.

With each troubling fox she discovered, she knew that a new story needed to be written on her heart in its place. So where did she go? She went to His Word to dive deep into the truth that would free her and allow her to reclaim her truest story—her origin story. The more she fed on His Word, the more His truth began to cry out from within and remind her of who He said she was. She paused to consume every word He had spoken. She allowed each syllable to pour over her and heal the places of fear, shame, and woundedness within her. She began to see clearly where the wounding messages, "troubling foxes," had taken root in her heart.

Rehearsing every word He had spoken to her in the secret place, His words began to change her from the inside out. They sunk deep into her soul, feeding the starved places, nourishing the forgotten spaces, and reassuring the most scared and insecure parts of her. She realized at that moment that nothing else mattered. She fastened His words to her heart, and this time she was not letting go. She would rise and face this mountain.

We Become What We Consume

I've come to realize that the longer I've walked with the Lord, the deeper the meaning of the word *flourish* has grown within me. As I've learned—sometimes kicking and screaming—to surrender to His slow, steady process, I've discovered that to flourish is to come alive again, especially in the places where life has left us feeling numb or depleted.

As we allow this sometimes very painful process to take place within us, we produce a beauty that is unsurpassed with power to change atmospheres and hearts around us! You see, other than freeing ourselves, there is another reason why gaining victory in our thought life is so important. Once we gain victory in our own mind and overcome strongholds, we are positioned to pull them down in the greater arena around us, in others, and in culture.

What we consume matters. And it turns out that the voice we listen to the most, becomes the voice that defines us. It is a battle we all face as believers. What voice are you listening to? The task before us is to learn how to live a life defined by Jesus's voice, our Bridegroom, and trust that He is the author of our story.

I love the thought of studying Scripture till it becomes you. But we must also realize that it isn't just what we consume but *how* we consume that matters. Are you consuming God's words with your head or your heart? The heart is mentioned eight times in Luke 8:5-18 as Jesus speaks about the parable of the seed. In verse 8, Jesus says, "Listen with your **heart** and you will understand." And in verse 15 He goes on to say, "The seed that fell into good, fertile soil represents those lovers of truth who hear it deep within their **hearts**. They respond by clinging to the word, keeping it dear as they endure all things in faith. This is the seed that will one day bear much fruit in their lives." Here is again in verse 18, "So pay careful attention to your **hearts** as you listen to my teaching, for to those who have open **hearts**, even more revelation will be given to them until it overflows. And for those who do not listen with open **hearts**, what little light they imagine to have will be taken away" (Luke 8:5-18, emphasis added).

When the bride finds herself questioning who He says that she is, she knows where to go. She knows what she must consume and how. She goes straight to His Word and allows it to soak deeply into her heart. She realizes it is the only place where her false story can be reimagined and rewritten. One of my favorite verses in all of Song of Songs is 6:6. The Bridegroom says, "The shining of your spirit shows how you have taken my truth to become balanced and complete."

As she feeds on His Word, something shifts within her. It is no secret that God uses words to create. From His very first "Let there be ..." He proved this true. God intended us to consume Scripture not just so that we would gain knowledge, but so that we would be transformed. This means we cannot remain in our head and transform our heart.

In *Praying the Psalms* by Daniel Henderson, the President of Strategic Renewal and Global Director of the 6:4 Fellowship, he and a team of pastors lead the reader through four movements within each Psalm.[3] These movements are based on how Jesus taught His disciples to pray through the Lord's Prayer and have the goal of helping Christian's experience "scripture-fed, Spirit-led, worship-based prayer." It has been a life-giving and renewing way for me to gleam from each Psalm a reassuring remembrance of the trustworthy character of God that is revealed. It has also allowed me to see more clearly the response that occurs within my own heart as I read the Psalm. It then directs me in how to pray and best prepare for the spiritual battle ahead of me. It has made the Psalms come alive for me in a whole new way, in a way that God intended all along.

God wants to speak your truest, most authentic story to your heart, and help you overcome any fear, doubt, pain or shame that is struggling to believe in how He sees you. And He will do that through His Word every time if we slow down enough to listen with our hearts. What old wounding messages within your heart are not allowing His Word to come alive in you?

Lectio Divina "Mining Deeper"

Let's end this chapter with an exercise to help us feed on God's Word from our heart. We need to allow our hearts to experience truth so that our stories can be reimagined through God's eyes, and to do that, we are going to glean from an ancient practice known as "Lectio Divina." We will learn how to mine the depths of God's Word and let it penetrate deep into our heart, not just our intellect. "Lectio Divina" is a Latin phrase that means divine or sacred reading.[4] I often think of it as mining deeper. It is a slowed down, heart-centered way of reading God's Word that helps us enter into a posture of receiving and become more open to encountering His heart. It's a way that we can live out Proverbs 4:20-22 which tells us to, "Listen carefully, my dear child, to everything that I teach you, and pay attention to all that I have to say. Fill your thoughts with my words until they penetrate deep into your spirit. Then, as you unwrap my words, they will impart true life and radiant health into the very core of your being."

As with most contemplative practices, this too begins with preparing your heart to receive. The steps that follow will lead you in a simplified version of this ancient practice:

Take a moment to quiet your mind, open your heart, and relax your body while taking a few slow, deep, and soothing breaths. Allow your senses to draw you into the present as you invite God into this space with you. Express your desire to hear from Him and ask that He reveal any needs you may be unaware of that your heart is holding. Choose a portion of Scripture to read and write it in your journal (Suggested Scriptures: Psalm 23; Psalm 27:1-8; Psalm 62:1-8; Isaiah 43:1-4; Isaiah 61:1-3; Matthew 14:22-32; John 10:1-6, Ephesians 3:14-20, Colossians 3:12-17).

- As you read the passage through the first time, pause to notice the words or phrases that seem highlighted especially for you. Which words or phrases are you drawn to and which ones do you find yourself resisting?

- Read it again and reflect on how these words or phrases apply to what you are experiencing in your life currently. How is God's heart pursuing yours through the highlighted words within the Scripture? In what ways is He revealing what is truest about you or helping you perceive the circumstances surrounding your life differently?

- As you read the text again or scan the highlighted phrases, listen for an invitation from God through the words you were drawn to or resisted. Start an honest conversation with Him about how you are experiencing His Word. In what ways did your heart come alive, feel seen, or experience hope? Or were there questions that arose, places of frustration that surfaced, or areas of confusion you experienced? Let your honest thoughts flow.

- Now as you lay your hopes, questions and even your frustration before Him, trust and rest in what you experienced through His Word. Know that He will continue to deepen it and reveal to you what your heart needs.

- Resolve to carry this experience with you into your everyday moments as you continue to mine deeper its meaning and seek how you are uniquely called to live it out. Think about how you can savor this experience with a symbol, phrase, or image you can keep with you as a reminder of what God revealed to you through this passage of Scripture. (Even a simple phrase on an index card will do).

Your wounding moments, wounding messages, and the defenses that formed are not the end of your story. There is a plot twist ahead. You will use this process and the revelation you received by practicing Lectio Divina to create another circle on the diagram we began in the last chapter. This circle represents the truth you now need to allow your heart to experience so that you can reimagine the story that got lost in the middle of your wounding moments.

Your Invitation to Feed on His Every Word

You are invited to rehearse His every word spoken over you. Let each and every one sink deep into the soil of your soul and bring to life your true identity. Hear Him say to you, "What devotion I see each time I gaze upon you. ... When I look at you, I see how you have taken my fruit and tasted my word. ... The shining of your spirit shows how you have taken my truth to become balanced and complete" (Song of Songs 4:1-2 and 6:6).

CHAPTER

7

Invitation 6 – Say Yes Despite Your Fears

D o you ever long to get away completely? Away from every pressure weighing you down, away from everyone and every voice vying for your attention? I try to practice this rhythm of retreat a few times a year. It's important to get away from the noise and distractions to let my heart hear more clearly what God is saying about how He sees me. It is a rhythm that helps me shift my human perspective and see my life and the things I am facing from His viewpoint. In the silence, stillness, and solitude, you also see your fears and insecurities more clearly and how they can easily cause you to compromise or settle back into comfort instead of calling.

Alone in the woods at a retreat center, I stumbled upon a beautifully landscaped, moss-draped labyrinth. As I entered, I noticed that my heart was heavy, full of questions and doubts. While walking the twists and turns of a labyrinth's path, it was easy to be reminded that life is also full of twists and unknowns ahead. I asked God, "Why does fear have to confront me at every new turn?" As I continued to walk in silence, I began to notice tree roots protruding within the path. When I felt them under my feet, I noticed they were sturdy, immovable, and oddly reassuring. Drawing me in with curiosity, I inquired, "Lord, what are you revealing to me in this moment?"

I sensed in the whisper of His heart that He was encouraging me not to focus on my fears, but on the roots. He said, "In the midst of the fear are the roots I've planted within you. These roots are yours completely and cannot be taken from you, uprooted, or moved. They are sturdy, sure, and planted by Me and no fear will ever have the power to uproot what I have placed within you." I walked out of the labyrinth with a completely new view gracing my horizon. Hope filled the space of my heart and I knew in that moment that there was beauty within me that no amount of fear could ever uproot.

It's important to recognize that fear is a natural part of every human story—it will surface, and it will need to be faced. I often find myself resonating with the story of Gideon, who needed multiple reassurances from God and laid out his fleece over and over. If we're honest, we've all been there—asking again and again, "Are you sure, God?"

Once Gideon fully grasped what God was doing through him, his obedience silenced his fear. When Gideon said yes despite a heart full of fear, his impact was extraordinary. Sometimes the bravest thing we can do is just say yes to the Lord and take a step in that direction—one step at a time of absolute surrender. This is God's invitation to us as He encourages us: "Say yes, dear, despite your fear. I promise the result will be worth it."

A Mind Made Up—The Shift

When I first began studying the Song of Songs, I knew within my heart that this part of the bride's journey was the most pivotal of all. This is where the shift within her happens, the shift that changed the trajectory of her destiny and clearly pointed her to her truest identity. I wonder if she even realized it was happening.

She finds herself saying, "I've made up my mind. Until the darkness disappears and the dawn has fully come, in spite of shadows and fears, I will go to the mountaintop with you—the mountain of suffering love ... Yes, I will be your bride" (Song of Songs 4:6). She knows there are things that must fall off of her, limiting stories she must no longer believe. She is ready to let go of the false self she created to receive love and believe in who God is creating her to be now. Her mind is made up! She gives Him her full and complete, "Yes!" She knows there will always be fears to face and obstacles to overcome, but something is different in her now. She is beginning to awaken to the paradise garden that He has planted within her. The gifts He gave her that can never be taken away. She must steward them now through her belief and choose to awaken fully to what is within her.

The moment she says yes, a transformation begins. A new identity emerges from Shulamite to bride. She awakens to what has been within her all along and for the first time in the entire journey, her true identity rolls off her tongue. She says at the end of verse six, "Yes, I will be your bride." When we say yes, we get a new identity and with that new identity comes a new story that we must now live out.

This invitation represents the fight of our life. The fight for our identity and the enemy of our soul doesn't give up easily. A battle is ahead for us as it was with the bride—the battle over which narrative we will believe. With the bride leading the way we must learn to accept our irreplaceable role that no one else can play. It is like every little girl's Cinderella story coming to life. So much came against her slipping into those shoes. So many negative messages causing self-doubt, even self-disgust to form within her. Then suddenly she caught the attention of a King, One who believed she was worthy of the role she never thought could be hers.

She had to overcome all the naysayers, especially the voices within her own mind to allow the shoe to be slipped in place. He, the King, was now asking her to walk out a completely different story, from a lowly nobody to the most important person in the King's life. The bride realized that the journey wasn't about how well she performed; it was about learning to embrace her worth through the King's eyes. In that moment, God revealed the truth of who she was—wanted, beloved, worthy, called. She understood that she didn't have to prove herself; she was enough simply by being herself, created in His image.

Saying yes requires that we put feet to the truth being planted within our heart. New ways of being and operating in the world will be required. To enter into the final leg of this steep climb, there is a universal action step every lover of God must take. It is one that will require deep resolve and intentional awareness. The false stories we've told for decades must leave our lips. We can no longer speak negatively of ourselves for it is the best way in for the enemy of our soul and destiny.

Archway of Trust

Living in a new story and believing we fit within its pages will require a whole new level of trust. Right after the bride declares her yes, the Bridegroom says, "Come with me through the archway of trust" (Song of Songs 4:8). I believe it is because He knew the battle that would be ahead of her and without trust the steep mountain terrain would be impossible to pass.

Three words sum up this chapter: identity, surrender, and trust. First, we say yes to our new *identity*, then we have to *surrender* our false story, and then *trust* that God will bring our new story to life. The Lord is targeting the issue of trust through this relational experience with His heart, because trust leads us into realms nothing else can. Through trust we can practice our new identity. The goal of placing your heart in His hands and reclaiming your identity is to transform the story within you—from one of fear to one of faith. Fear and love will always be in contention for your heart. Which story will you listen to? Which will you trust?

We see here that the Bridegroom does not take her trust in Him lightly (Song of Songs 4:7-11). He wants to make sure she understands what her devotion has done to His heart. Her brewing trust and love for Him moves Him deeply as He is undone by her worship. Her hand in His fills Him with overflowing joy. We often focus on what God's love does to us, but do we ever stop to think about what our love does to the heart of God? Thinking about what I do to the heart of God stirs something deep within me. Pause to notice what it may stir in you.

Not only does the Bridegroom want the bride to see how her heart impacts Him, He wants to make sure she understands and sees the full potential of that which resides within her heart. The Bridegroom knew this would be hard for the bride to fully grasp. He begins to describe the nine fruits of His Spirit that He has been cultivating and growing within her all along. He tells her, "Your inward life is now sprouting, bringing forth fruit. What a beautiful paradise unfolds within you. ... for many clusters of my exquisite fruit now grow within your inner garden" (Song of Songs 4:13-14).

One of the best descriptions of the nine fruits found within the bride I have come across was in the book *Journey Into Intimacy* by Christy Hill.[2] Christy describes the Song of Songs with such depth and beauty and the way she speaks of this moment with the Bridegroom is unmatched. She says the Bridegroom looks into the Bride's eyes and says, "Instead of the hidden, covered, and restricted life you have come to accept, the abundance you are finding in me will offer hope to multitudes. Deep wisdom and understanding will flow through you as a pure stream of water. Its source is my own heart. My life will flow out through you into a dry and thirsty world." What a beautiful picture of God describing the depths of the bride's soul and saying to her, "for I find the Promised Land flowing within you" (Song of Songs 4:11).

He goes on to describe nine "exquisite fruit" that now grow within her inner garden (Song of Songs 4:13-14). Nine is significant because it represents the presence of the Holy Spirit cultivating and stirring to life these inner qualities. In studying this portion of the Songs, my heart was overcome. The beauty that unfolds next as these fruits are described requires an open heart to fully grasp.

- *Pomegranates* lead the way. If you have ever opened a pomegranate, the first thing you see is a burst of color with a multitude of dark reddish seeds scattered within. Pomegranates Biblically represent an open heart of love that is filled with passion. From the very first seed planted within her, the Bridegroom is showing her that she has counted herself as insignificant, but has a love and passion within that has the potential for greatness. Therefore, pomegranates represent the "unlimited" and "unprecedented fruitfulness" that God has placed within those who love Him!

- *Henna* comes next. It comes from the root word "ransom" or "redemption price" and reminds us of God's mercy.[3] Christy describes the meaning of this fruit within the bride powerfully when she says, "the bride carries within her the sweet scent of henna, imparting the fragrance of forgiveness and the beauty of reconciliation wherever she goes."[4]

- *Spikenard* follows and is a very rare and costly perfume. It symbolizes the outpouring of the bride's heart to the one she loves. It has also been known to mean light. She is light as He is light.

- Next is *Saffron*. In Biblical times, it was recognized and highly regarded for its many healing properties. There is an emphasis here that healing is within the Bride.

- *Calamus* in Biblical times was a trade item used to make incense and perfumes. It was also one of the five ingredients in the anointing oil used in the tabernacle (Ex 30:23). Christy points out that calamus "is a picture of the covenant God makes with His bride...it is a symbol of the Lord's promise to come to us, to fill us with His presence and dwell with us forever."[5]

- *Cinnamon* was yet another exotic and costly spice found in the garden within the bride. It was used as a sweetener for food and had an attractive scent. What the bridegroom is saying about the bride with this fragrant spice is that she is beautiful and sought after.

- *Frankincense* comes next and highlights the bride's purity of heart and the spirit of thankfulness and worship stirring within her.

- *Myrrh* was used in Biblical times as an anointing oil and consecration to God. It represents the suffering love of Christ and speaks of a heart full of trust.

- *Aloe* comes last. It was known as the "medicine plant" and its healing properties were highly regarded in Biblical times. As Christy points out, "The presence of both saffron and aloe indicates that healing for every kind of disease and illness belongs to the bride."[6]

I can't help but soak in the unsurpassed beauty, rarity and value that all of these spices found within the bride's inner garden represent. Isn't that who God is though? There is no one better than Him at reminding us of our unmatched beauty and worth. Trust begins here; with believing in the paradise garden God has carefully crafted and cultivated within your heart. He has intentionally placed within you everything you need to fulfill the story He has written for you. Believing this allows us to gain entrance to and inhabit a place few ever see. The depths of God's heart holding ours with eyes of pure honor and delight. This realization is what led the bride to pray a brave and bold prayer.

The "Do Whatever it Takes" Prayer

The bride finally believes she has something of value within her. This story began with "let him" love me, and now it shifts to letting Him taste of the fruits within her so that His plans will be fulfilled through her, no matter the cost. She prays:

> Breathe upon me with your Spirit-wind. Stir up the sweet spice of your life within me. Spare nothing as you make me your fruitful garden. Hold nothing back until I release your fragrance. Come walk with me as you walked with Adam in your paradise garden. Come taste the fruits of your life in me. (Song of Songs 4:16)

She knows that there is still work to be done within her heart. Just because she said yes doesn't mean the internal battle no longer exists. And secondly, maybe most important of all, she references the garden of Eden. Eden in the Bible is a picture of walking and talking with God, of intimacy that is open and transparent. Eden is the setting where relationships flourish. She is recognizing that she cannot do this alone, nor was she ever meant to.

We get a glimpse here of the final chapter. The ultimate goal at the end of this journey is to learn to live a life defined by God's voice and entwined with His heart. She repeats this prayer just a few sentences later when she says, "Come walk with me until I am fully yours. Come taste the fruits of your life in me." What a shift from "but I am so unworthy" in the very beginning to "come taste the fruits of your life in me" now.

What Are You Saying YES to?

Over and over I have sat with women, asking them about the longings in their soul, and watched as they shrink away. They dismiss, deny, or all together neglect that a longing exists. Why does it come so easy for us to deny? Do we fear selfishness? Do we fear inadequacy? Do we fear there is nothing really of value within us and that we were somehow the only one God missed?

What has the world and our experiences programmed into our souls? Remember, Scripture says, "Even before we were born, God planned in advance our destiny and the good works we would do to fulfill it!" (Ephesians 2:10). Could you really be the only one God excluded?

The truth is, there is a stirring in each one of us, unique to each heart—a beating, a rhythm all our own. Why is the truest thing about us also the thing we fear the most? There is unlimited fruitfulness and potential within us and yet, we struggle to believe it. I've seen it, woman after woman, not believing in what is within her. Have you found yourself there too? If we confronted the thoughts of inadequacy and not enough-ness out loud, would they make as much sense in light of God's heart for us written on every page in His Word?

We find the answer in Song of Songs 1:4 when the Shulamite says, "Draw me into your heart" and "We will run away together."

She is saying, "I want more of you Lord. Let's do this. I want to fulfill the life vision you have for me. I want to minister with you from this place of deep connection with your heart." You see, there is a disconnect and dissonance in our soul when the two things every believer wants remain unfulfilled—intimacy and mission. Both are written deep within our souls and need expression. We often try to do one more than the other, or neglect one in favor of the other. When we do, our soul withers and our ministry suffers.

We must learn to run and rest well. One without the other simply doesn't work. All service for God must flow out of intimacy with Him. Here lies the crossroads in all of our journeys. We either stay the same and settle, or we go deeper and discover the true longings within—the longings that cry out when no one is watching, the longing that can't be denied yet we silence all the time because of fear. You will only see this longing clearly when alone with the Maker of your heart.

The Feeble First Steps

What story is God trying to release within you? What do you need to be open to in order to allow your heart to experience what your wounded messages convinced you was unattainable? What first feeble steps will lead you in the direction of reclaiming the story God has written for you? James Clear, the popular author of *Atomic Habits*, explains, "Your life today is essentially the sum of your habits ...What you repeatedly do (i.e. what you spend time thinking about and doing each day) ultimately forms the person you are, the things you believe, and the personality that you portray."[7]

My encouragement to you is to take the first step. Write the first sentence of the book in your heart or the song you've longed to sing. Take the first course, training, or class. Start doing what the person you long to become would do and just keep putting one foot in front of the other. Do as David did when he said, "Here's what I've learned through it all: Don't give up; don't be impatient; be entwined as one with the Lord. Be brave and courageous, and never lose hope. Yes, keep on waiting—for he will never disappoint you!" (Psalm 27:14).

I feel like I am living out this invitation right now in so many areas of my life. From being a writer and constantly having to convince myself to put my words out there into the world, to being a ministry leader and having to network and believe in what I am providing. Each day it is just one foot in front of the other, doing what writers and ministry leaders would do. I don't always get it right. Far from it friends, but one thing I know is I will not give up. I will be brave. I will say yes in the face of my fears, and I will keep going. Because I know God is there ready to hold my hand, reassure me of who I am, and lead me every feeble step I take.

Build an Altar

If you find yourself in this wrestling match of identity as I so often have, maybe it is time you built an altar. Take the time to create space for a ceremonial moment where you come before the Lord and abandon your false story, creating an opportunity where you can lay down your unbelief. Confront your troubling foxes of compromise, comparison, self-criticism, self-doubt, defense, and complaining, especially when it comes to being self-critical and speaking negatively about yourself.

Pause to imagine who you would be free to become if you allowed your heart to be fully rooted in God's love and no longer let fear, doubt, or insecurity hinder the view of your truest and most authentic self. I've always loved the phrase "still becoming" because we are all works of art in progress. And the more we envision our truest selves, the greater our chances are of becoming her. Take a leap with your pen. Write down who you want to become. What is the truest version of you doing? What is she saying? What fear is she facing? The clearer you see her and believe she has been within you all along, the more she will come to life.

Write a letter to her, describing her in great detail. Research has shown that people who are more in tune with their future self do a better job of taking care of their present self so that they can say yes to becoming the person they were designed to be all along! So don't hold back: imagine the characteristics your future self possesses, what she is free to do, and then back it up with Scripture. Craft the version of yourself that is living truest to all your passions, dreams, and desires. What is she like? How does she hold herself? How does she show up? How does she tend to her inner world in a way that allows her to fully flourish? Let your imagination run wild.

Write a letter to yourself for five days in a row. Then at the end of the week, notice the themes that emerge. Use your reflections to write down actionable steps that you can do to move closer to this ideal version of yourself in the present moment. What can you do today? Use whatever time you need to fill up a page or two in your journal each day. Then, do as one of the loveliest mentors in my life taught me to do: reread the truths and the things you are saying yes to every day. Begin your morning speaking life into your true identity. Record it and take your morning run with it ringing in your ears. Let it wash over your soul each and every day because again, the more you envision her, the greater your chances of becoming her.

Once you have a clearer vision of her, pull back out the circle diagram we began in chapter five. Remember how I said God will not leave us here, stuck in our old limiting narrative? This is where our story shifts. Draw a final circle around the automatic defenses you identified earlier (See Figure 2 for an example). And begin to fill in the outermost circle with both truths from God's Word and the small steps of faith you are saying "Yes" to that will allow you to live differently and rewire in new patterns. Opening our hearts to new experiences is what allows us to change. Let's catch those troubling foxes, feed on His truth, and say yes to the new things God has in store for us.

It is possible to heal and begin to capture the beliefs that have long held you back. By feeding on God's Word and perspective, His truest story for you can be reclaimed. Then seeped in a new view, you will find the courage to say yes to who He says you are. It does take time. It does take intentionality and it does take peering into places you may have long avoided. But I will say this: healing has never been a choice between pain or no pain. On one end, we are choosing the pain of staying the same and preserving what is broken, or on the other end, we are choosing the pain of transformation.

Both have a cost. But I would rather choose the pain that gives birth to something new than stay with the pain that keeps me stuck in patterns that re-wound my heart over and over. Eventually our wounds and wounded messages will demand our attention. May we bravely turn toward our hearts and hurt, giving them the attention they lovely deserve so that transformation can begin.

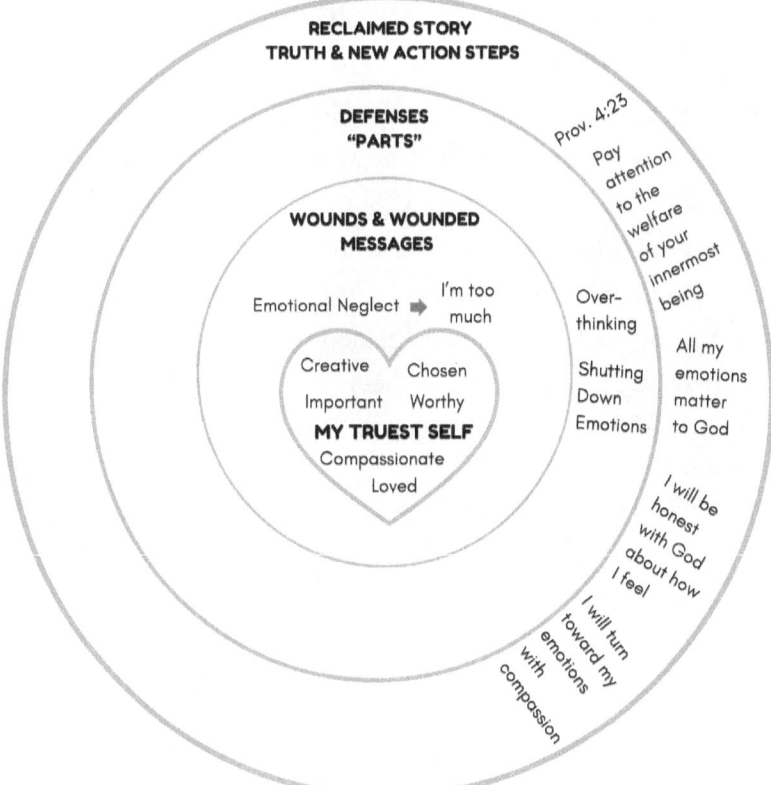

Figure 2 illustrates a full-circle healing process. It begins at the center with a reminder of who you are. Here you can add some of the words/phrases that arose in writing your letter to your most authentic self. Next, we see an example with naming the wound as emotional neglect, which gives rise to a wounding message: *"If I feel my feelings, they'll overwhelm me—I'm too much."* In response, a protective defense develops—over-intellectualizing and shutting down all emotions—to avoid the pain of being perceived as "too much." From there, healing begins by identifying a truth from God's Word and taking a clear action step: choosing to get honest with yourself and connect with God in moments where you are feeling overwhelming emotions, rather than shutting down or escaping into your thoughts. This shift starts to reshape a new, healthier pattern—one rooted in emotional honesty, spiritual connection, and the freedom to feel without fear.

Your Invitation to Say Yes Despite
Your Fears and Doubts

You are invited to fully trust in who God is for you and in what he has planted within you. Say YES to what He has for you, no matter the doubts and fears that surface. Shift away from the doubting lie that you don't have what it takes to the truth that He has planted beauty within your soul that is meant to be shared with the world. May this be your prayer: "I've made up my mind. ... in spite of shadows and fears, I will go to the mountaintop with you——the mountain of suffering love" (Song of Songs 4:6).

Third Leg

Reveal His Heart - Be Entwined

Now that you've braved the inner depths of your heart, you can confidently live out your truest story as His beloved and reveal His heart to the world.

The third leg of this journey will inspire you to reveal God's love to the world through the unique passions and desires within you. You will find He has been uncovering and revealing the truest you, every step of the way. The final three invitations create the possibility of living a life entwined with God's heart.

Transformed by the Bridegroom's heart, the bride was compelled to go out and reveal to the world the same love she received. This now becomes our journey. We, too, must learn how to receive His love and let it shape who we become, as well as the story we accept about ourselves. Then, and only then, are we able to fully reveal the depths of His heart to others and give what we first received. The three invitations within this final leg of the journey will ask you to:

Cultivate the Nevertheless Mindset
Spur Each Other On
Live Entwined with His Heart

CHAPTER

8

Invitation 7– Cultivate the Nevertheless Mindset

"The question is not, What will I have to give up to follow Jesus? but rather, What will I never get to experience if I choose not to follow Jesus? The answer is clear: we will forfeit the chance to live a good and beautiful life."

– James Bryan Smith

L et's be honest—life with people can be both beautiful and overwhelmingly hard. If you've ever poured your heart into ministry or leadership, you already know: some of the deepest wounds come from those you've loved, led, and trusted most. These experiences can shake us, wear us down, and if left unhealed, can tempt us to close off our hearts entirely.

In pouring out my life in service to others, I've encountered rejection, faced unexpected betrayal, and felt deeply drained by the constant expectations and demands placed on me. In situations where the odds seemed impossible, I have struggled to believe in God's ability and promise to work *all* things for good in my life. And though it is hard to admit, I ran into the arms of false saviors: jobs, titles, accomplishments, and people. I busied myself with creating temporary solutions that brought fleeting moments of ease to my discomfort. In my emptiness, thirst, and ever increasing burnout, I reached out to sources that couldn't sustain me, and weren't meant to.

The most painful trials we face often involve relationships. When I've been hurt by others or distracted by challenges that overwhelmed me, I've found myself trying to devise a *"Plan B."* Before I even realized it, I had created faulty solutions that led me further away from God's story for my life. Harsh betrayal and deep wounding resulted in unacknowledged anger toward God, and I ran to other sources for answers. Ultimately, I ran *from* the truest version of me. I spent years running from her, but no matter how far I went, something in me knew she was always there just waiting for me. God tenderly and gently kept drawing me back home to her. His pursuit was faithful and unwavering, determined to bring the truest version of me back to life.

God says in Isaiah 55:3, "Pay attention and come closer to me, and hear, that your total being may flourish. I will enter into an everlasting covenant with you, and I will show you the same faithful love that I showed David." What is His invitation to us here? Just a few short verses before, He says, "Listen! Are you thirsty for more? Come to the refreshing waters and drink." He is reminding us where we find refreshment and nourishment when our souls have become parched by life. He is saying: "Come to Me, hear My heart, so that everything within you that has been deadened can come to life again." He longs to be the oasis in the desert our souls are desperate for, and when we come to Him, He makes us a promise like no other: *I'll make a covenant of steadfast, sure love with you that can never be broken.*

It is only the certainty of God's steadfast love, securing our every step, that makes the final leg of this journey possible. Here, we face a steep climb—one where we can easily find ourselves settling for safer ground, going through the motions half-heartedly, or walking away entirely. We've all felt the ache of our once fiercely shining light dimming, and we wonder how we ended up there. I believe part of the answer is found in chapter five of the Song of Songs. And, what it reveals is the key to running our race with both tenderness and strength intact.

Here, we're invited to deepen our unwavering belief in the identity God has been whispering to our hearts in the secret place. As we continue the journey, intimidation will likely rise as a familiar foe—so there's a mindset we must intentionally cultivate. A *nevertheless* mindset: one rooted in defiant perseverance, unshakable resolve, and fierce determination to keep moving forward, no matter what challenges arise.

It's time to enter the deeper depths of God's heart, where we learn not only to endure suffering but to flourish in the midst of it. The question before us is this: *Will we stay faithful to the call on our lives when things get hard, when disappointment runs deep, and when the way forward seems impossible?*

Deeper Still

There is a life-altering revelation for us here in chapter five of the Song of Songs. The Bridegroom begins by saying, "All of the fruits of my life I have gathered from within you, my paradise garden. ... My life within her will become your feast" (Song of Songs 5:1). Every time I read this, it amazes me how He sees us. Her heart and life have become so connected with Him that Jesus is saying here, "If you taste of her, you are getting Me."

Shockingly, right after this mountain peak moment, we find the bride saying in verse two, "After this I let my devotion slumber ..." Up until this point, she had been facing her fears and growing in service and devotion to Him, and then this sudden change of heart. We aren't told what specific experiences she had, but we can all imagine what may have transpired. When you've poured your heart out in service to others and wound up wounded, what was your response? I've been there, wanting to hide away and stop the bleeding by never putting myself out there again.

But even in this moment where her passion fades, there is a part of her heart that is still beating. She goes on to say, "But my heart for him stayed awake." I have often said in the midst of painful moments when things have gone in a direction I never expected, what else would I do? The alternative just won't work. There is a part of me that longs to love like Jesus, and it remains lit, no matter what life brings. No matter how many times the world has tried to snuff it out, the longing to reveal His heart drives me to stay in the fight and keep loving. Light is within us all. Nothing life brings can ever take it from us. It can dim it, try to diminish it, but it can never fully blow it out.

Here again we see the Bridegroom come to her, no matter what state she is in. She says, "I had a dream. I dreamed of my beloved—he was coming to me in the darkness of night. ... I heard his knock at my heart's door as he pleaded with me" (Song of Songs 5:2). He came to her in this dark, despairing place. In her moment of need, He knocks on the door of her heart saying one of the sweetest lines in all of the Song of Songs, "Arise, my love. Open your heart, my darling, *deeper still* to me. Will you receive me this dark night?" (Song of Songs 5:2, emphasis added). We see a similar verse in Revelation 3:20 where God is saying to His bride (us), "Behold, I'm standing at the door, knocking. If your heart is open to hear my voice and you open the door within, I will come in to you and feast with you, and you will feast with me." Can't you just see Him standing outside the door of the bride's heart, of *your* heart, knocking? Asking, "Will you receive Me and the love and comfort I want to give you?" In the moments we've been devastated by life and people, He sees. When we pour out repeatedly and find ourselves hurt, depleted, blindsided and weary, He comes to the door of our hearts knocking.

How does the bride respond? Not in the way we might expect—and if I'm honest, I've responded the same way. She says, *"You have cleansed my life and taken me so far. Isn't that enough?"* (5:3, emphasis added). He is calling her deeper still—into more of His presence, more of His love—but she settles for less. She chooses plan B and begins looking elsewhere for comfort. We do this, too. We turn from God and reach for something external, something more tangible to soothe the ache within. Maybe it's shopping, sweets, overworking, or seeking affirmation from others.

But comfort is not what we find.

The bride goes searching, but instead of solace, she encounters pain: "As I walked throughout the city [which often symbolizes the church or community] in search of him, the overseers stopped me as they made their rounds. They beat me and bruised me until I could take no more. They wounded me deeply and removed their covering from me" (Song of Songs 5:7). She finds herself wounded by people and circumstances she never expected. Blindsided and confused, she stumbles around trying to make sense of what happened. The bride's story gently reminds us that seeking what only God can provide in places He never intended often leaves us more wounded. Yet, even in that place, His love does not retreat. The invitation to return remains.

During one of the darkest times in the bride's life, a major shift occurs. She reconnects with an enduring and deep resolve within her, giving her the courage to stay the course. She utters the most powerful words her heart has ever spoken: "Nevertheless ... if you find my beloved one, please tell him I endured all travails for him. I've been pierced through by love, and I will not be turned aside!" (Song of Songs 5:8). Nothing mattered more in that moment than reconnecting with her Bridegroom and living out the story He had written for her.

She decides things have to be different this time; she can no longer live and believe as she once did and move into the fullness of who she is meant to be in Him. Unlocking her heart to Him while wrestling with fear and heartache led to a profound realization. God was not outside of her needing to be found, He was within her all along just waiting for her to receive Him. She resolved in her heart to cultivate the "nevertheless mindset" and believe that no matter what life brings, He is there. Always there. She surrenders to His faithful leadership and recalls all the ways He has shown up for her along this journey deeper still into her heart where He dwells.

Can you believe that even in the trials and wounding moments you don't understand, God's love is doing all that is necessary to lead you on the path to a flourishing life? Do you hear Him knocking at the door of your heart? Will you allow Him to enter? We must come to trust that there is a table for two that is set in our hearts. He is just waiting for us to come and sit so that we can flourish in His presence.

How Do We Cultivate a Resilient Mindset?

Resilience is not a characteristic only some people possess; it is a skill that can be learned. Flourishing in harsh conditions is evidence of resilience. As the bride's story reveals to us, there are certain things resilient people do. There are ways of perceiving and thinking that allow the "nevertheless mindset" to take root within us.

Resilient People Acknowledge Suffering as a Normal Part of Life

First and foremost, resilient people know and embrace that suffering is a part of life. Author and psychiatrist Curt Thompson is clear to point out in his book, *The Deepest Place,* that "all suffering shares common attributes, most important is the reality that we all suffer, even if we are often quite extraordinarily unaware of it."[2] Then why is it so hard for us to turn our suffering into resilience? He says:

> In fact, the culture in which we live has trained us to become increasingly fragile. Research on the development of resilience suggests that successive generations over the last forty years have found themselves less and less able to be hopeful about the future because they lack the interior emotional and relational architecture necessary to do so.[3]

Denial of suffering doesn't make it not exist; it just makes us less resilient when we experience it. During training sessions with teachers on cultivating resilience, I emphasized that one of the biggest obstacles to developing resilience is failing to recognize the impact that life experiences have had on us. One of my life's purposes is to help people understand how negative experiences have shaped them into who they were not meant to be, allowing them to become who they have always been designed to be. When we recognize that tough times are a normal part of being human, it helps us to realize we are not alone or discriminated against by life in any way. But it also allows us to give ourselves permission to name how we have been adversely impacted and then respond to it in healthier ways.

Resilient People Cut Ties With Plan B

When we hold on to *"Plan B,"* we never fully commited to *"Plan A"* did we? It is as if we have one foot on both sides of the fence, just in case we need to turn back. Essentially, we are saying, "If God's plan for my life doesn't work out, if He doesn't come through for me, I have an alternative." Have you ever found yourself riding that fence? I sure have.

But one thing I've learned is this: in order to be resilient in the craziness of this life, I can't have a *"Plan B."* We can't go higher if we are tied to and restricted by our lesser plans. If God has called you to something more, you have to cut the rope. I believe we all are given a "for such a time is this" Esther moment that cannot be denied. There is something only you can give the world. We have to fight to remember our why and what legacy we want to leave. So often, we let fear and discomfort make us retreat or shrink down the size of the greatest longings that burn within us and we settle. May we learn to be a people who are all in, where the challenges we face make us stronger, instead of convincing us we must have heard God all wrong.

It is time we quit pretending to be all in. There is no going back. We've got to cut the rope to any alternative plan if we want to climb higher into all God has for our lives.

Resilient People Accept Responsibility for Their Progress or Lack Thereof

I remember a writing coach and mentor of mine once telling our group you can either, "blame, shame, or play the game." It is easy to fall into the trap of blaming others and circumstances when life hurts, is uncertain, and hasn't panned out in all the ways we had hoped. One thing I want to certainly clarify is we don't dismiss the hurt, we acknowledge it—but we suffer when we continue to hold onto resentment and bitterness. At times, anger is a very valid response when we have been mistreated or hurt by others. Anger is often an indicator that a boundary we hold has been crossed; it's important to turn toward it, not suppress it. But there are also times where we hold onto resentment and bitterness struggling to forgive for way longer than a heart should ever hold. The goal is to get to a place where the things that offend us don't knock us out of the game.

Secondly, when we feel we've messed up royally or aren't where we'd like to be by now, it can be easy to slip into a shame-based spiral. I have yet to meet a person who shamed themselves into becoming the person they wanted to be. Personally, I suffered for way longer than I needed to after my father's death, because in the midst of the most painful experience of my life, I made some bad decisions that

I couldn't seem to forgive myself for. God lovingly helped me to see that I could turn to myself with kindness and let it go. He already had a long time ago.

Perhaps the suffering we experience from blame and shame can be eased. We can learn to play the game no matter how hard, while letting go of bitterness and freeing ourselves from the prison of shame. Therefore, the best option we have is to decide to play the game. To not quit. To realize it is going to be dang tough. There will be moments when you question if you have what it takes, and are hurt by people you never expected, but don't you dare quit.

Resilient People Know Where to Focus Their Attention

Those who are more resilient focus on what they can change. They also have a tendency to do what resilience expert, Dr. Lucy Hone, described as "hunting the good stuff."[4] As most of us know by now, our brains default to noticing threats and finding the negatives around us more often than the positive due to survival instincts. Recognizing threats around us is crucial for living a longer life. While it's important not to ignore these threats or dismiss our emotions, we should also be intentional about focusing on the positive aspects of our lives.

Two ways to center your focus into a more resilient way of operating is to first ask yourself, "Is what I'm doing healing or harming me?" It is important that we bring awareness to our habitual patterns that do not serve to heal us but just continue the suffering. Second, learn to ask more "what" questions and less "why" questions. Why questions only show us our limitations; *what* questions help us see potential all around us. *Why* questions are great at stirring up negative emotions; *what* questions allow us to remain curious. *Why* questions trap us in our past regrets; *what* questions help us experience hope. Indeed, making the transition from *"why"* to *"what"* can be the difference between feeling powerless and being empowered. Simply shifting from, "Why is this happening to me?" to "What can I do about it?" automatically puts us in a space where we can become more resilient, curious, and uncover more possibilities.

Resilient People Know the Value Within Them

Resilient people embrace the beauty that resides within them. We have to stop living as if greatness isn't already within us and believe what Jesus says, in John 14:23: "My Father will love you so deeply that we will come to you and make you our dwelling place." In 2 Peter 1:3, we are told of an unbelievable reality: "Everything we could ever need for life and godliness has already been deposited in us by his divine power." Everything we need to live our most authentic story and flourish in this life has already been placed within us. What keeps us from accessing it? Belief.

We have to stop believing the lie that we aren't enough or that we can earn value through our performance. Self-sufficiency is a myth at best and a prison at worst. God's presence with us, "Emmanuel," and within us was never designed to be something we had to earn. It has always been something to be openly received.

Resilient people recognize their inherent value and practice self-compassion. They respond to suffering and setbacks with kindness toward themselves. To grow in both intimacy and ministry, we must stop speaking negatively about ourselves and begin to believe in the worth of what lives within us.

Resilient People Trust in God's Mercy and Goodness

"Surely goodness and mercy shall follow me all the days of my life" (Psalm 23:6, NKJV). I go back to this famous ending in Psalm 23 anytime I feel in doubt of God's plan over my life. It is no coincidence that right in the middle of the bride's story, the Bridegroom asked her to go through the archway of trust with Him. Without trust, it is impossible to move further up the mountain and into an entwined life with Him. The greatest quality we can grow in if we want to cultivate the nevertheless mindset is trust—trust in God and His ever-flowing goodness.

In James, we are encouraged to "count it all joy" when we face trials:

> My fellow believers, when it seems as though you are facing nothing but difficulties, see it as an invaluable opportunity to experience the greatest joy that you can! For you know that when your faith is tested it stirs up in you the power of endurance. And then as your endurance grows even stronger, it will release perfection into every part of your being until there is nothing missing and nothing lacking. (1:2-4)

This is one of the greatest promises in all the Bible. In the middle of a trial when we praise and place our hope in His truth, we become people who can endure any circumstance. We become balanced and complete, lacking nothing! If we believe that He truly works all things for good (Romans 8:28)—no matter the circumstance, hardship, or pain—then we can experience joy in expecting His goodness to come. Sometimes in situations where I find my heart is breaking and I just don't understand, I simply say out loud, "I trust you, Lord," even when I don't feel it. Because the cost of not trusting is just too steep.

While not exhaustive, this list highlights some of the most essential mindset shifts we can begin to cultivate in pursuit of a truly flourishing life. As I close this section, I want to emphasize something important: though relationships can bring some of our deepest challenges, they are also among our greatest assets. When it comes to resilience, the strength of our relationships and support networks is the most critical factor. That's why I've dedicated the entire next chapter to exploring it. Stay with me—what comes next may forever change the way you view connection.

A Resilience Building Practice

One of my favorite resilience-building practices is simply remembering and reflecting on God's faithfulness. Throughout Scripture, we're reminded to do this often—because we are so prone to forget. We see the bride in Song of Songs practicing this very act in one of the darkest moments of her life. Onlookers questioned her, asking, "Why do you love him? Couldn't someone else do?" It would've been easy for her to agree and walk away. But she didn't. Instead, she began to recall all the reasons she loved the Bridegroom, listing the ways He had pursued her and remained faithful to her (5:10–15). As she remembered, her heart was filled with courage—and even the doubters began to desire what she had.

Here's my challenge to you: *make a list of all the reasons you love Jesus and all the ways He has pursued you, been faithful, and proved His trustworthiness to you over the years.* Then pull out your list in moments where you are finding it hard to trust in His goodness and read it as a reminder of His faithfulness. May this practice infuse your heart with courage when you need it most.

The Apostle Paul did this so well. What better encourager is there than him? Paul, while in prison and while potentially enduring one of the darkest moments of his ministry life, penned these words in Philippians 1:

> I pray with great faith for you, because I'm fully convinced that the One who began this glorious work in you will faithfully continue the process of maturing you until the unveiling of our Lord Jesus Christ! (vs 6) ... I continue to pray for your love to grow and increase beyond measure, bringing you into the rich revelation of spiritual insight in all things (vs 9). ... I want you to know, dear ones, what has happened to me has not hindered, but helped my ministry of preaching the gospel, causing it to expand and spread to many people (vs 12). ... No matter what, I will continue to hope and passionately cling to Christ, so that he will be openly revealed through me before everyone's eyes. So I will not be ashamed! In my life or in my death, Christ will be magnified in me (vs 20). ... Whatever happens, keep living your lives based on the reality of the gospel of Christ (vs 27). ... For God has graciously given you the privilege not only to believe in Christ, but also to suffer for him. For you have been called by him to endure the conflict in the same way I have endured it—for you know I'm not giving up (vs. 29-30).

Your Invitation to Cultivate the Nevertheless Mindset

You are invited to no longer be tossed about by circumstances but instead be determined in your heart to trust no matter what life brings. Fully let go and surrender your whole heart, trusting that God is faithful, true, and always does what is best for you. May this be your prayer: "Nevertheless, I will endure all for him. I've been pierced through by love, and I will not be turned aside!" (adapted from Song of Songs 5:8).

CHAPTER

9

Invitation 8 –
Spur Each Other On

"Discover creative ways to encourage others and to motivate them toward acts of compassion, doing beautiful works as expressions of love. This is not the time to pull away and neglect meeting together..."
- Hebrews 10:24-25

Recently, I woke up feeling curious about an odd dream I had. Over the years, I've learned to pay attention to distinct moments in dreams that I recall vividly. This dream was long and full of details, but there was one specific part that attracted my attention. In the dream, my mother handed me a handwritten note in my father's handwriting. It read, "Write a sermon about pickles." (Weird, right?) The word *PICKLES* was in large letters. So, what did I do? I got up and started looking for metaphors related to pickles.

It turns out there's a surprising depth to the symbolism of pickles. I found metaphors for transformation, preservation, social immersion, purity, and flavor enhancement. One that particularly stood out described how we start out as cucumbers, get immersed in pickle juice, and are transformed into pickles or become "pickled."

The pickle juice represents culture, society, norms, expectations, and the people around us. I would even add religion and family into the mix, as those first interactions highly influence how we are shaped. The issue often arises when society mistakenly blames the cucumber—ourselves—while ignoring the pickle juice—our environment, especially when it comes to trauma. This is likely because focusing on it being solely the cucumber's fault gives us a sense of control. The truth, however, is that when you're immersed in something day in and day out, it will inevitably shape and change you. Most of the time, we don't realize how deeply it's impacted us, because it's all we've ever known. This is where redemption comes in. There's one ingredient in the pickle juice that stands out: salt.

In Matthew 5:13-14, we are told to be two things in the world for others: salt and light. Jesus says, "Your lives are like salt among the people. ... Your lives light up the world." The presence of salt in the pickle juice changes everything. Salt preserves and protects. It inhibits the growth of harmful bacteria and promotes the growth of good bacteria. It prevents spoilage and ensures purity. The right amount of salt brings out the best in the pickle, enhancing its flavor.

Salt is a simple, seemingly insignificant thing, yet it's anything but small. Jesus is the salt in the pickle juice. He knew that the pickle juice (the world and our experiences) would impact us, and He had a plan for redemption all along. Jesus came to redeem and restore us knowing fully what the world would try and do to us. We are not condemned by the pickle juice we were soaked in; we are preserved, protected, and strengthened by the salt—by Jesus. He came to make us resilient. He knew that our hearts would inevitably be impacted and even wounded by the world around us, so He made a way for our redemption.

There were a few other insightful things I learned about salt in Biblical times that I never knew, which highlight what we should be for one another. For example, salt was used to treat wounds—makes sense, right? There was also something called a "covenant of salt," a symbol of an unbreakable alliance between God and His people, representing friendship, loyalty, and commitment. Salt was even used on the wick of a candle to enhance its brightness, and further symbolized value, purity, hospitality, and new beginnings. The most profound realization came as I reflected on all this: Jesus was the salt for us, and now we are called to be salt for each other. This is what a healing community is all about. We need to create safe spaces where we can openly recognize how the pickle juice has shaped, harmed, and even distorted our view of ourselves. If we don't understand the influence of the pickle juice we were seeped in and bring compassion into the scene, we become pickled—jaded and bitter. And worst of all, we become false versions of ourselves stuck in limiting stories.

That's where we come in for each other—resilient people know they can't do it alone.

Over the past two decades as a counselor, I've become convinced that our greatest source of resilience as humans lies in the strength of our relationships. We are to be preservatives in each other's lives—loyal, committed to growth, and radically hospitable. We help prevent the growth of harmful influences in those we come alongside and encourage the growth of what's good. We are the medicine—the salve for each other's hearts in a world that hurts. Through it all, our goal is not to resign to the influences of the pickle juice, but instead, to enhance each other's unique flavor and encourage each other to stay salty—never hiding our light again.

Living a Life of Influence

Even while still in one of the darkest moments of her life, the bride declares, "If you ask me why I love him so, O brides-to-be, it's because there is none like him to me. Everything about him fills me with holy desire! And now he is my beloved—my friend forever" (Song of Songs 5:16). Her unwavering love and "nevertheless" mindset were on full display, and it stirred something in those watching. Drawn to the light within her, they responded, "We long to see him too. Where may we find him? We will follow you as you seek after him" (Song of Songs 6:1).

She feasted on His presence—and then became a feast for others. No longer ashamed of her story, she found the courage to inspire. Knowing that no one heals alone, she became determined to build a community marked by acceptance, warmth, and invitation—so others could encounter His transforming love. For His love had completely undone her fears. Now, she longs for others to experience what she has: a love that invites, restores, and makes whole. She beckons them in, just as God once welcomed her, hoping they, too, will embrace the truth she's come to know—that we are worthy of the story God has written for us.

It makes me think of Jesus as He encouraged His disciples during His last moments on earth. He prays for them and His future church saying, "I have revealed to them who you are and I will continue to make you even more real to them, so that they may experience the same endless love that you have for me, for your love will now live in them, even as I live in them!" (John 17:26).

Instruments of Repair: A Call to Collective Well-being

In the world of trauma and attachment, an important relational concept we highlight is the idea of *rupture* and *repair*. Every relationship, no matter how healthy, experiences moments of rupture: those disconnects, misunderstandings, or misattunements that cause emotional pain or distance. And no matter how hard we try to avoid it, when we experience these relational ruptures, they require relational repair. It is in the repair that we grow more resilient.

Unfortunatly, I see the weight of unrepaired ruptures every day in my counseling work. Most people who walk into my therapy office are carrying around a collection of ruptures that have never been tended to, never acknowledged, and never healed. Those unhealed wounds are affecting their ability to regulate emotionally, to feel safe in relationships, and to live resiliently.

Some ruptures are obvious and painful, but many are small and subtle—what we call *"micro-ruptures."* These happen every day, often without us recognizing the toll they can take. Just the other day, I cheerfully greeted a new coworker as I passed by her office. She didn't look up from her phone. No smile, no wave—just a short "hey" back. I instantly felt my joy deflate. I was trying to connect and make her feel welcome, but instead, this fleeting interaction led to micro-rupture between us. It made my mind whirl with questions about what I may have done wrong. The problem with these seemingly minor slights is they build up over time, especially when they go unaddressed and can affect all future interactions with that person.

The more attuned we become to these moments, the more we can begin to tend to the ruptures within us and be mindful of how we might unintentionally contribute to them in others. The problem is we've gotten really good at burying these moments of rupture and we wonder why the mental health crisis around us continues to grow.

But God is serious about *repair*.

We see it throughout the entire Biblical narrative—and especially in the Song of Songs. In the previous chapter, we witnessed Jesus, the Bridegroom, running after the Bride, knocking gently on the door of her heart in an effort to repair the rupture that had taken place. But she turns away, seeking comfort elsewhere. That only leads to more pain, more disconnection, and more relational wounding. These kinds of relational ruptures can cause us to pull away not only from people, but also from God—the very Source of the healing our hearts so desperately need. To live a flourishing life, we must bravely allow our hearts to be repaired, so we can become *repairers* rather than sources of further pain.

So why do we resist repair? Because it costs us something. It takes effort, humility, and vulnerability—things we often prefer to avoid. We become like non-compliant patients in a spiritual hospital. Jesus, the Great Physician, stands ready to heal our wounds. He invites us to the table of healing—but too often, we squirm our way off the operating table, fearful of what repair might require. The question is: Will you allow repair to happen within you—so you can become an instrument of repair in the world?

Learning to love well is what becoming more like Jesus is most about. Community takes intentional work because it can be messy and hard. How do we love well even when it costs us something? I think we all know we need connection; what we don't realize is what gets in the way. There is an art to connecting in a way that brings healing, and with intention and awareness, it's something we can all cultivate.

Before moving on, take a few quiet moments for reflection. Use the questions below to guide your journaling. If we truly want to become instruments of repair, we must begin by becoming aware of what might be standing in the way of others experiencing us as a safe, compassionate, and healing presence.

- Where have I experienced recent relational ruptures—big or small? (Consider both obvious wounds and subtle, unspoken hurts.)

- Can I ask for help without fearing being a burden or feeling like I have to be the strong one for everyone else and it isn't okay for me to have needs?

- Are there moments I've minimized or ignored that might still be affecting me emotionally or spiritually?

- Are there moments I've been guilty of not being attuned or fully present with someone else's story or pain?

- In what ways might I have unintentionally caused a rupture in someone else's life? (This is not about shame, but about becoming more aware and intentional in your relationships.)

- What keeps me from allowing God or others to see the tender places in me that require repair? (Fear, self-protection, pride, or perhaps past experiences of being hurt when you reached out for help.)

- What do I personally need to feel safe in community with others?

- In what ways do I long for my heart to be seen and supported?

- What would it look like for me to say yes to the healing work of repair—in my own heart and in my relationships so I can be an even greater source of healing for others?

The Art of Connection

"The happiest and healthiest people are those who have warm connections with others," says psychiatrist Robert Waldinger, who leads the Harvard Study of Adult Development.[1] It is the world's longest scientific study on happiness. This study, which has spanned eight decades, consistently shows that relationships are the key to a happy, healthy, and resilient life.

If I haven't convinced you yet how important our level of connectedness is, let me go on the record and say that relationships are the number one resiliency factor we have as humans to overcome the stress, trauma, and hardship we all encounter in our lives. Psychiatrist, Dr. Bruce Perry, highlights this in his book *What Happened to You?* when he says, "Our ability as people to tolerate stress is diminishing because our connectedness is diminishing."[2]

He then expressed his concern about what he calls the "poverty of relationships" in our modern society and how in all his research they found that, "the best predictor of your current mental health is your current relational health, or connectedness."[3]

The more disconnected we become not only with others but with ourselves, the more the necessary skills we need for connecting deeply are fading. Together let's explore what key qualities are needed to create healing communities and healing interactions.

Psychological Safety

The number one thing present in healing spaces is safety. Our nervous systems are scanning for cues of welcome or warning every second of every moment of every day whether we are aware of it or not. According to Google's Project Aristotle, a multi-year study of 180 teams across various departments revealed that **psychological safety**—a climate where team members feel safe to take interpersonal risks—is the single most important factor for team effectiveness.[4] Psychological safety also refers to an individual's perception of the consequences of taking those interpersonal risks. It is a shared belief held by the members of a team that it's okay to express one's ideas and concerns, speak up, and admit mistakes—all without the fear of negative consequences. These negative consequences which plague most of us in social interactions are fears of being seen as flawed, ignorant, incompetent, not having it all together, or being misunderstood.

In spaces where psychological safety is high, individuals feel safe to take risks around others. Essentially their nervous systems feel cues of welcome to be themselves and they are confident that when they share their viewpoint they will not be judged, embarrassed, or shamed, no matter what they bring to the table.

I was reflecting on how psychological safety can play out socially after a training I attended on the Polyvagal Theory in clinical practice. It was refreshing to listen to people in a crowded room who felt completely free to be honest about how their individual nervous system was responding moment by moment without fear of shame or judgement. The facilitator intentionally created a welcoming, safe space to explore and express themselves. I wonder what the world would be like if we were freer to speak the language of the nervous system and not feel like we have to hide, deny, or dismiss what we are experiencing.

Our nervous systems are always being shaped in the direction of more resilience or less. If we had more spaces of psychological safety and welcome, we could stop putting on a smile when something feels off inside. If we were less judgmental of our natural responses and more accepting of our human experiences, we would be better able to tend to our emotions without piling on shame or fear. We are not superhuman. If we want to be resilient, we must stop pretending that nothing affects us. Constantly feeling like we have something to prove harms us. Imagine how much safer and more connected we would feel if we could be completely honest. For without safety, there can be no true connection.

Self-Awareness and Relational Mindfulness

Self-awareness—knowing who we are and how we impact others— is another vital quality in healing spaces. However, only 10-15% of people possess true self-awareness, according to organizational psychologist Tasha Eurich.[5] Fortunately, it can be cultivated, and it turns out there are two key aspects that need to be fostered: internal and external self-awareness.

To build healthy communities, we must both know ourselves deeply and practice relational mindfulness. Before we speak—especially when we hold influence—we should pause and ask, "How is what I am about to say going to *feel* like to the person hearing it?" Too often, we speak to soothe ourselves rather than to support others. When we struggle to sit with our own emotions in healthy, accepting ways, we are less likely to be experienced as supportive. But the more we learn to listen to ourselves with curiosity and compassion, the better equipped we are to extend that same presence to others.

Corrective Emotional Experiences

As we learn to develop external self-awareness it leads to the next essential quality of healing communities. Thriving communities provide corrective emotional experiences—moments of repair where our worst fears are disconfirmed. For example, if I fear that my voice won't be heard, but in a group, I am surrounded by compassionate listeners who value what I have to say, something shifts in my nervous system. This happens when what was predicted gets disconfirmed by the compassionate response of those around me. Therefore, the skill of listening well to understand, not just be understood, will always be essential in healing spaces.

One of the most painful forms of loneliness isn't being alone—it's feeling unseen and unknown in a room full of people. It's the ache of being surrounded yet still invisible. When those around you don't truly hear you or understand the essence of who you are, it can feel like you're slowly fading—like your presence is shrinking into the background until you're no longer sure you even matter. We can play a part in changing this experience for others by providing corrective emotional experiences that increase the resilience and well-being of those around us.

Co-regulation

As humans, we have an ongoing need for co-regulation—the way one nervous system can soothe, shape, and stabilize another. Being a healthy co-regulator in someone's moment of need isn't about having the perfect words. It's about *presence*. It means showing up as a safe, compassionate, and non-judging presence—someone who can hold space and simply *be with* whatever the other person is experiencing. Because we are wired for connection, our emotional states are deeply contagious. My nervous system will affect yours, and yours will affect mine. The way we show up for each other has the power to calm or to intensify what's unfolding.

Clinical social worker, Deb Dana, explains, "The ability to self-regulate is built on ongoing experiences of co-regulation. Through co-regulation we connect with others and create a shared sense of safety."[6] This means we are always asking, "Will you be there for me?" and "Can I be safe with you?" We were created to need each other, but for many, healthy co-regulation was not readily available, so rugged self-reliance was developed instead. Learning to be a safe co-regulator for those whose relationships were more harming than healing is one of the most life-giving ways we reflect God's love in community.

Savoring the Good

Finally, one of the beautiful traits of healing communities is their intentional practice of savoring the good and celebrating even the smallest steps forward. Because of the brain's natural negativity bias, we often overlook the subtle but significant shifts happening in our growth. Taking time to acknowledge and reflect on progress—not just in ourselves, but in others—cultivates hope. Many of us struggle to see the good in our own journey and need the loving perspective of others to remind us how far we've come.

Pausing to celebrate small victories nourishes our souls and strengthens our collective resilience. It's in these moments of shared joy and intentional gratitude that healing deepens and hope is sustained.

This is by no means an exhaustive list of what makes a healing space, but my hope is to highlight the essential qualities needed for safe and meaningful connection. May we grow ever more courageous in our pursuit of being known, seen, and fully loved. In the end, the reward of vulnerability far outweighs the risk. We both give and receive the gift of being truly seen and understood—and only then can everyone in the room experience genuine belonging. The truth is, the very vulnerability we fear holds the power to bring deep connection and lasting healing.

Healing spaces offer a safe environment to practice new ways of being. We all have habitual patterns that hinder our growth, and we need others to help us see what we can't. Asking for help is one of the bravest things we can do. As we grow in emotional intelligence, we embrace our neediness and develop the courage to be vulnerable.

I hope you find the courage to seek out psychologically safe spaces—places where you can truly be vulnerable. If meaningful connection is the greatest contributor to mental health, then fear of vulnerability may be the greatest barrier to flourishing and overcoming life's stressors. Without vulnerability, there can be no growth. When we disconnect from our authenticity out of fear that we won't be accepted, we end up being afraid to be ourselves. That's why one of the most powerful gifts a healing community offers is the courage to rediscover who we truly are—and the safety to live fully into our most authentic stories.

Your Invitation to Spur Others On

You are invited to become a feast for others. Hold nothing back, give the gifts He has created within you to the world, and inspire others to see the unique gifts within them. Build or join a community of like-minded believers where you can be seen, known, loved, and grow stronger together. Hear Him say to you, "All the fruits of my life I have gathered from within you_____, (your name) ... My life within [you] will become [their] feast" (adapted from Song of Songs 5:1).

CHAPTER

10

Invitation 9 – Live Entwined with His Heart

"Who is this one? She arises out of her desert,
clinging to her beloved."
— Song of Songs 8:5

My husband and I love exploring new hiking trails together. I've realized I'm not exactly a fan of hiking alone—but when he's with me, I feel bolder, more confident, and ready for the adventure.

One morning, while walking an unfamiliar path, I felt anxiety begin to rise in my chest. I've learned over time that wherever there's tension, it's worth paying attention. As the trail twisted and turned, so did my thoughts: *Should we keep going? Turn back? Is this even the right way?* There was a quiet hesitancy—an irrational little worry that we might somehow get lost for good. As I stumbled along trying to look casual (and not like someone internally spiraling), it hit me: this hike felt *a lot* like my journey with the Lord. Unfamiliar path. Some hesitation. Lots of trust. And thankfully, someone much more capable walking with me the whole time.

We naturally want to know what lies ahead, but the path often winds into a distance we can't yet see. In His grace and wisdom, God doesn't reveal the entire journey—only the next step we're ready to take. Honestly, if He had shown me everything I'd face in ministry and life before I was prepared, I probably would have turned and run the other way. But somehow, by His strength and gentle discretion, I've stayed in the fight.

Sometimes, gaining a sense of control feels like the answer to our fears—I know I've fallen into that trap more than once. That morning on the trail, I found myself longing to know what was waiting around each curve, how steep the next hill would be, and how long it would take to get back to familiar ground. My thoughts began drifting toward fear—mostly irrational, but distracting all the same. And in that distraction, I struggled to stay present to the very thing I needed most: God's steady, guiding presence right beside me.

I'm proud to say there were a few moments along the way when I allowed myself to pause and take in the awe: my eyes tracing the height of a tree reaching into the sky, and a quiet little exchange with a deer frozen in surprise at the sight of me. There was beauty along the path—beauty I would've missed if I had been focused only on reaching the end.

Clearly a park ranger had gone before, created the path my feet were trodding, and it was safe. Why then the questions and the doubt? I've always believed God is the Maker of my path, I just don't always trust I'm on the right one or that I won't take a wrong turn. King David in a moment of heaviness expressed to the Lord, "My strength was sapped, my inner life dried up like a spiritual drought within my soul" (Psalm 32:4), and he heard the Lord respond, "I will stay close to you, instructing and guiding you along the pathway for your life. I will advise you along the way and lead you forth with my eyes as your guide. So don't make it difficult; don't be stubborn when I take you where you've not been before. Don't make me tug you and pull you along. Just come with me!" (Psalm 32:8-9). I think God wrote this about me.

I often wonder when I'll fully allow myself to be immersed and mesmerized by His knowing and my blind trust. I've had enough experiences to know that the Carver of my path can be trusted to never let go of my hand, make sure I have moments of delight along the way, faithfully lead me to exactly where I need to be, and make me bolder. In Him, I find the confidence to climb higher and become a voice and a light that reveals His nature. Psalm 25:4-5 perfectly sums up my prayer for you as you continue around each uncertain bend: "Direct me, Yahweh, throughout my journey so I can experience your plans for my life. ... Escort me into your truth; take me by the hand and teach me. ... I have wrapped my heart into yours."

From the very first encounter with the bride-to-be, the Bridegroom King—Jesus—was lovingly setting the stage for her entire journey. Every step, every moment, was drawing her deeper into the truth of her identity. *In the end, the one who flourishes has discovered her truest self reflected in His eyes and has entwined her heart with His.* All along the way He has unconditionally, unquestionably loved her and taken her gently by the hand, leading her back home to her truest self. This is the invitation: to be fully known, deeply loved, and forever changed in His presence.

Isaiah 40:31 beautifully describes this deeper still, entwined life: "But those who entwine their hearts with Yahweh will experience divine strength. They will rise up on soaring wings and fly like eagles, run their races without growing weary, and walk through life without giving up." The Maker of our hearts beckons us to entwine ours with His, and as we do, we reveal His heart to the world. The Message version of Ephesians 4:6, my life verse, captures the heart of my deepest prayer so eloquently when it says, "Everything you are and think and do is permeated with Oneness." Yes, Lord; may all I do and say be permeated with *oneness* and led by your heart and Spirit.

A Transformed Heart

As they are nearing the peak of the mountain together, the Bridegroom says, "The shining of your spirit shows how you have taken my truth to become balanced and complete" (Song of Songs 6:6). Each step was a choice she took that drew her deeper into His heart and closer to the revelation of her truest self. Yet, within her, there was still a question left unanswered. She says, "Why would you seek a mere Shulamite like me?" (Song of Songs 6:13).

Isn't it so easy to fall back into doubt? His response floods my soul with courage, proving yet again how trustworthy, faithful, and endearing He is. He reminds her first of her status, saying, "You are truly royalty! ... the poetry of God—his very handiwork. Out of your innermost being is flowing the fullness of my Spirit—" (Song of Songs 7:1-3). He continues to pour His heart out in verses three through nine, expressing the harvest ready to come forth within her, and how her "life stands tall as a tower, like a shining light on a hill" (Song of Songs 7:4). She has a new level of discernment as He describes her thoughts as being "full of life, wisdom and virtue" (Song of Songs 7:5). He tells her about the delight she brings Him and how her beauty is unmatched. Again, His loving reassurance does not fail to bring her into a state of complete awe.

With His healing words poured once again into her soul, she is now bolder than ever. She declares, "Now I know that I am filled with my beloved and all his desires are fulfilled in me" (Song of Songs 7:10). She has walked with Him into the deepest places of her heart, and allowed Him in to clear out what didn't belong: the lies, the wounds, the false narratives. Again and again, He reminded her of her true identity. He fought for her, stayed with her, and patiently helped her see herself through His eyes—until she could arise, clinging to Him. Now she knows who she is—no questions, no doubts, and no longer needing reassurance from anyone else.

This revelation gives the bride the courage to invite her Bridegroom to go to the forgotten places. She no longer fears the cost or the discomfort that being His love in the world may bring (7:11). She knows that her journey will always be one of growing, maturing, and becoming more like Him and that it will require things of her she didn't even know she could do. But she also trusts that something within her has been deeply changed.

With that assurance, she knows she never walks alone. They are one—ascending the mountain of suffering love, united in purpose and vision. Together, they will go after the forgotten. She knows she is here for a reason, and that truth burns within her. Her heart can no longer deny it. Standing tall, her head held high, she is no longer swayed by doubt. Every part of her is fully embraced by all of Him. She has become a tower of strength, a living picture of true confidence.

Joining her Bridegroom in a divine duet, twirling on the mountaintop—she is a light for all to see. She has become a radiant reflection of His presence in the world. Looking at the mountain that had once felt so daunting, a smile of confidence spreads across her face. She has been sealed with His fiery love, and no amount of pain or persecution will ever be able to extinguish it (8:6-7). She was made for this moment; to dance in the high place of the sky, united as one (8:14).

Surrendered Trust

One of the most inspiring verses in the entire Song of Songs is found in 8:5: **"Who is this one? She arises out of her desert, clinging to her beloved."** What moves me most is that she doesn't arise in her own strength or through sheer effort—she arises *clinging to her Beloved*. That image captures this entire journey so beautifully. And yes, I know I've said it before—but like God often does in Scripture, I feel the need to repeat it: the bride's willingness to say *yes* to His every invitation made all the difference. Because at the heart of it all, what was truly at stake was her belief in her truest identity.

From the very beginning—back in chapter one—we started with Love's invitation: to rediscover your truest self, the one who has been there all along, waiting to be seen through the eyes of Love. The climb we've taken together—the mountain we've been scaling—is all about arising into your identity in Christ. Every step of the way, He has been whispering: *"This is who you are. This is how I see you."* The journey *deeper still* is about letting that truth sink into the very core of who we are—until it becomes not just something we know, but something we live and breathe.

In the end, what gave the bride the strength to arise in this way? She placed her full trust in Him—even when the path was unfamiliar and the places He led felt uncertain. Trust became her turning point.

As I studied and read and reread chapters seven and eight of the Song of Songs, I began to see that the entwined life is a life lived in surrendered trust. When I looked up all the synonyms for trust, something began to stir in me, for all the qualities of trust perfectly describe our Redeemer King. It is only through trust that we can rise from the wilderness moments of our lives and ascend to the highest places with Him. To trust God means we fully believe in who He is within us. It means placing our whole confidence in His character, resting in His faithfulness, and depending entirely on His strength, truth, and goodness. Trust is more than belief—it is assured reliance. It is knowing deep in our soul that He is unchanging, unwavering, and always true to His promises. He is our future hope. In Him, we can confidently expect that every promise will be fulfilled. We commit our way to Him, placing our lives in His tender, capable hands. For in Him, we find all we've ever longed for: confidence, reliability, certainty, assurance—and freedom from fear and doubt.

If trust is the entryway into the entwined life, how then do we learn to trust? We trust by becoming rooted. More than anything else, this journey has highlighted our desperate need to be rooted in God's love and for His view of us to become our fierce reality. We are coming back full circle to Paul's prayer that started it all in Ephesians 3:17: "Then by constantly using your faith, the life of Christ will be released deep inside of you, and the resting place of his love will become the very source and root of your life." This is how we overcome the fears that plague us by staying entwined with His heart and becoming rooted in His love. Let's take a moment now to review the journey we have traveled together thus far and use the acronym "rooted" to help us remember the invitations we've been asked to accept along the way:

Rest in His loving presence. Every journey deeper into God's heart begins with rest. We stop, pause, and still our hearts in His presence so that we can...

Open our hearts to receive His words spoken over us and soak in His love and delight. We bravely become vulnerable and receptive so that we can...

Observe our inner landscape in complete honesty. We name what is within us, hiding nothing. We give voice to our emotions and thoughts and confront the troubling foxes that have sought to rob us for way too long. We observe with curiosity and compassion our inner world so that we can...

Turn to God's heart for truth. We seek to discover what God's love is asking us to embrace about how He sees us so that we can...

Experience His truest most authentic story for our lives. We let His truth sink deep into the soil of our soul with brave action steps in order to allow the false story we've been believing to be rewritten so that we can...

Determine in our heart to believe in what He has placed within us. We face life and all it brings with a deep resolve; the "nevertheless mindset" that says every step of this journey has been for our good to bring us into the fullness or our identity in Christ. Then and only then can we reveal His heart to the world.

In Isaiah 41:9-10, God makes a promise to His people—to us, His Bride. He says:

> I drew you to myself from the ends of the earth and called you from its farthest corner. I say to you: ... I have chosen you. I have not rejected you! Do not yield to fear, for I am always near. Never turn your gaze from me, for I am your faithful God. I will infuse you with my strength and help you in every situation. I will hold you firmly with my victorious right hand.

We must now decide how we are going to respond. Will we surrender in complete trust and allow our hearts to be entwined with His?

Your Way Home

Your truest identity is this: you are God's beloved. Your destiny is to live in the freedom of that truth, carrying His love into the world. When we truly believe we are His beloved, it sets us free to love others with confidence—uniquely and authentically, just as He designed us to.

When endeavoring anything new, anxiety and fear will always greet us. Afterall it is risky to offer up ourselves into a world where so many things seem to move against us. When I reflect on the mental health struggles affecting our world today, I can't help but wonder if they stem from a common source: the inability to freely express our true selves. There is an inner turmoil that arises from knowing there is more to us while feeling trapped in a false narrative. We have to acknowledge the longing within us and stop suppressing our true selves.

As I pondered this truth of being His beloved on a walk one morning, I began listening to a song I'd never heard before called "Made for Jesus" by John Mark Pantana and Olivia Dyer. [1] I stopped dead in my tracks when I heard them sing, "The whole point of my existence is to know your love, the whole point of my existence is to know you Lord." My instant response was, "Yes, Lord, I want to know Your love so that I can give it away." But then I heard His gentle whisper and a greater revelation surfaced: "Josie, it isn't about what you can do. The entire journey really is about knowing Me so that you can see yourself as I see you and open your heart deeper still to My love." Everything we do for Him will flow from this space of being loved without any effort, striving, or performance. I can't say I have fully arrived here, but I'm on my way.

As I continued my walk that morning, I found myself overcome with gratitude. I reflected on all those who had gone before me who were brave and faithful enough to put out into the world what was in their heart. Because of them, my life was changed. They inspired me to grow, push forward, and keep fighting. I'm sure you, too, if you paused in this moment, could bring to mind someone you are unbelievably grateful for—a person who overcame their fears to put out into the world words, a song, a picture that forever changed you. By them being free to be themselves, it set something free within you that you weren't even aware was chained.

Now, it's our turn to pick up the torch. The blank canvas at the center of our being is waiting, and we are called to become a light in the darkness for others. Our lives may have taken twists and turns we didn't wish for, and we may have chosen a path of pain or two because of those sudden twists and turns. But all the while, there has been a plan of redemption. God's love has been and always will be pursuing us to guide us back home to our truest selves.

The thought that there is a garden God has placed within each of us that may never be tended to saddens me. It is one of the main reasons I wrote *Deeper Still*. It is for all those untended to gardens of possibility and promise that my words bleed onto this page—to encourage you that you matter and everything you long to be is within you.

I invite you to walk with me into one last reflective moment as we end this journey together. The physical act of walking a labyrinth is an experience I have adored over the years. Some of the most moving moments within my heart have been while walking the twist and turns of its path in silent reflection. The entrance represents the journey of your life so far. You approach with an open heart, eager to discover where God has been guiding you and how your journey has shaped and transformed you. Your intention is to settle deeply in your heart, where God patiently awaits to greet you.

In the middle, soaking in His presence and growing in trust is where things begin to be transformed within our heart. We are able to see the possibility of a new story and walk out differently. Changed. With a pep in our step, we walk the same path out in which we came, but we are not the same as we entered. As we leave, we have a confident trust in who we are designed to be in the world, because we know the overflow of His heart is now pouring out of ours.

The bride entered this journey fearing, as I believe all of us do, that she was unworthy of His call. She was fearful she wouldn't measure up, that she didn't have what it takes. The bride who entered the labyrinth was consumed by a false story shaped by the painful moments of her life, but the one who emerged was confident and a tower of strength for others, barely recognizable from the trembling legs that once entered. When I think about the bride's journey to the center of the labyrinth (or her heart) this is where the turning point of her life occurred. She met the Bridegroom in the deepest place within her, and it was there where His story began to unfold and shifted how she saw herself. As she soaked in His presence and built a foundation of trust, she was able to walk out of the center of her heart with a head raised in full confidence. She was now fully entwined with His heart and she knew, she just knew what she was made for.

So, what will your next step be? I encourage you to imagine yourself entering the labyrinth within your heart. Thinking about how you began this journey and all the twists and turns your life has taken to bring you to this moment. How has God been shaping you all along for this next season of your life? As you enter the center of your heart, you find a blank canvas and with this canvas, you have the opportunity to co-create a new narrative with God. Let me ask you: What will the world miss if you don't trust the story He's painting for you? Who will be left unchanged if you let your fear of inadequacy win?

Who is the woman walking out of the labyrinth now? What are you designed to give the world? Take her in because she is beautiful. I am sure and certain the garden within you is beaming with unprecedented fruitfulness—planted by the One who made you to carry a fragrance that transforms those around you. His presence overflowing from within you is the gift you now give to others. I encourage you to go after His story for you. Do something that stirs up the wonder and awe within you. Ask Him, "What do you want to do together, hand in hand?" **You were designed to flourish in His presence.** He is asking you now, "Can I have this dance?" He extends His hand to you and you find yourself on the mountain top wrapped in His embrace, dancing to the truest melody written for you without shame, without fear, without doubt. You are her. Suddenly free to become the truest version of yourself in a way that you never thought was possible!

Your Invitation to Entwine Your Heart with His

You are invited to believe that God is not outside of you in need of being found, but within you, empowering your every move! Listen as His heart rejoices over the progress you've made. You have made the climb, faced your fears, silenced your doubts, and found the courage to become the woman God sees! Hear Him say to you, "The shining of your spirit _____, (your name), shows how you have taken my truth to become balanced and complete." And may this be your declaration: "Now I know that I am filled with my beloved and all his desires are fulfilled in me" (adapted from Song of Songs 6:6 and 7:1, respectively).

Chapter Notes

Introduction

1 Soots, Lynn. quoted in Ackerman, Courtney E. "What Is Flourishing in Positive Psychology?" *Positive Psychology*, 9 May 2018, https://positivepsychology.com/flourishing/. Accessed 21 July 2025.

2 Simmons, Brian. *The Passion Translation: Song of Songs.* BroadStreet Publishing Group, LLC, 2017, 286-287.

3 Hall, Todd, and Elizabeth Lewis Hall. *Relational Spirituality: A Psychological-Theological Paradigm for Transformation.* InterVarsity Press, 2021, 2.

4 "Restoration of the Soul." *Bible Hub*, www.biblehub.com/topical/r/restoration_of_the_soul.htm. Accessed 17 June 2025.

Chapter 1

1 "Flourish." *Encyclopedia.com*, www.encyclopedia.com/literature-and-arts/performing-arts/music-history/flourish. Accessed 17 June 2025.

Chapter 2

1 Simmons, Brian, and Candice Simmons. *The Sacred Journey: God's Relentless Pursuit of Our Affection.* BroadStreet Publishing Group, 2015, 6.

2 Young, Sarah. *Jesus Calling: Enjoying Peace in His Presence.* Thomas Nelson, 2004, 234.

3 Jesus Culture. "Living With a Fire." *Let Love*, Jesus Culture Music, 2018.

4 "Let." *Dictionary.com*, www.dictionary.com/browse/let. Accessed 17 June 2025.

5 Simmons, *The Passion Translation: Song of Songs*.

6 De Mello, Anthony. *Sadhana: A Way to God*. Image Books, 1978, 120.

7 Simmons, *The Passion Translation: Song of Songs*.

8 Neff, Kristin D. "The Elements of Self-Compassion." *Self-Compassion*, www.self-compassion.org/what-is-self-compassion/#the-elements-of-self-compassion. Accessed 17 June 2025.

9 Manning, Brennan. *A Glimpse of Jesus: The Stranger to Self-Hatred*. HarperCollins, 2003, 94.

Chapter 3

1 Muller, Wayne. *Sabbath: Finding Rest, Renewal, and Delight in our Busy Lives*. Bantam, 1999, 20.

2 Robbins, Mel, host. "Dr. Gabor Mate: The Shocking Link Between ADHD, Addition, Autoimmune Diseases, & Trauma." *The Mel Robbins Podcast*, 21 November 2024, https://www.melrobbins.com/episode/episode-235/.

3 Nagoski, Emily, and Amelia Nagoski. *Burnout: The Secret to Unlocking the Stress Cycle*. Ballantine Books, 2019, 6.

4 Nagoski and Nagoski, *Burnout: The Secret to Unlocking the Stress Cycle*.

5 Barton, Ruth Haley. *Invitation to Solitude and Silence: Experiencing God's Transforming Presence*. InterVarsity Press, 2010, 16.

Chapter 4

1 Barton, *Invitation to Solitude and Silence: Experiencing God's Transforming Presence*.

2 Mona, Brittany. "Toxic Positivity: Examples and What to Say Instead." *Forbes Health*, 2 August 2023, www.forbes.com/health/mind/toxic-positivity/. Accessed 28 June 2025.

3 Paschall, A. *Feel: A Collection of Liturgies Offering Hope for Every Complicated Emotion*. Bethany House, 2024.

4 Paschall, Anjuli. "Don't fear, really feeling: How your emotions are key to unlocking real hope & connection." *Ann Voskamp Blog*. September 2024,

https://annvoskamp.com/2024/09/dont-fear-really-feeling-how-your-emotions-are-key-to-unlocking-real-hope-connection/.

5 Siegel, D. J. *The Mindful Brain: Reflection and Attunement in the Cultivation of Well-being*. W. W. Norton & Company, 2007.

Chapter 5

1 Scazzero, Peter. *The Emotionally Healthy Leader: How Transforming Your Inner Life Will Deeply Transform Your Church, Team, and the World*. Zondervan, 2015.

2 Perry, Bruce D., and Oprah Winfrey. *What Happened to You? Conversations on Trauma, Resilience, and Healing*. Flatiron Books, 2021.

Chapter 6

1 Cooke, Graham. "*The Prophecy of Scripture*." *Brilliant Perspectives Podcast*, 5 October 2023, https://www.brilliantperspectives.com/podcasts.

2 Bethel Church. *Choose Your Stronghold*. YouTube, 30 September 2020, www.youtube.com/watch?v=PmIGJi6bSw8. Accessed 20 June 2025.

3 Henderson, Daniel. *Praying the Psalms: Experiencing Scripture-Fed, Spirit-Led, Worship-Based Prayer*. Strategic Renewal, 2017.

4 Barton, Ruth Haley. "Lectio Divina: Engaging the Scriptures for Spiritual Transformation." *Transforming Center*, July 2019, https://transformingcenter.org/2019/07/lectio-divina-engaging-the-scriptures-for-spiritual-transformation-2/. Accessed 21 June 2025.

Chapter 7

1 Cummings, E. E. *E. E. Cummings: A Miscellany Revised*. October House, 1965.

2 Hill, Christy. *Journey into Intimacy: A Study in the Song of Solomon*. WestBow Press, 2015.

3 Hill, *Journey into Intimacy*, 124.

4 Hill, *Journey into Intimacy*, 124.

5 Hill, *Journey into Intimacy*, 128.

6 Hill, *Journey into Intimacy*, 130.

7 Clear, James. *Atomic Habits: An Easy & Proven Way to Build Good Habits & Break Bad Ones*. Avery, 2018.

Chapter 8

1 Smith, James Bryan. *The Good and Beautiful LIFE: Putting On the Character of Christ*. InterVarsity Press, 2009.

2 Thompson, Curt. *The Deepest Place: Suffering and the Formation of Hope*. Zondervan Books, 2023.

3 Thompson, Curt. *The Deepest Place: Suffering and the Formation of Hope*, xvi.

4 Hone, Lucy. "The Three Secrets of Resilient People." *TEDxChristchurch*, August 2019, https://www.ted.com/talks/lucy_hone_the_three_secrets_of_resilient_people.

Chapter 9

1 Rocha, K. "The Secret to a Happy Life – Dr. Robert Waldinger (TED Animated)." Robert Waldinger, 23 October 2024, https://www.robertwaldinger.com/post/the-secret-to-a-happy-life-dr-robert-waldinger-ted-animated.

2 Perry and Winfrey. *What Happened to You? Conversations on Trauma, Resilience, and Healing*, 255.

3 Perry and Winfrey, *What Happened to You? Conversations on Trauma, Resilience, and Healing*, 258.

4 "Google's Project Aristotle." *Psych Safety*, 28 Mar. 2004, psychsafety.com/googles-project-aristotle/. Accessed 29 June 2025.

5 Eurich, Tasha. *Insight: The Surprising Truth About How Others See us, How We See Ourselves, and Why the Answers Matter More Than We Think*. Currency, 2017.

6 Dana, Deb. *Polyvagal Exercises for Safety and Connection: 50 Client-Centered Practices*. W. W. Norton & Company, 2020.

Chapter 10

1 John Mark Pantana, featuring Olivia Dyer. "Made for Jesus." *YouTube*, uploaded by John Mark Pantana, 20 September 2020, www.youtube.com/watch?v=cnz1ZUNObjA. Accessed 30 June 2025.

About the Author

Josie is a Licensed Professional Clinical Counselor specializing in trauma and resilience. As the founder of *Shine Healing Ministries*, Josie leads women through transformative experiences focused on rest, restoration, and encountering God's heart in deeper ways. With a heart for holistic well-being, Josie is deeply committed to creating safe spaces where faith and mental health can intertwine. Her ministry and counseling practice reflect a commitment to walking alongside others as they overcome their fears, develop inner resilience, and embrace their authentic story.

www.ingramcontent.com/pod-product-compliance
Lightning Source LLC
Chambersburg PA
CBHW031515120626
46545CB00005B/1895